The Forgiving Church

Sue Curran

The Forgiving Church

Library of Congress Catalog Number 90-81814

ISBN 1-56043-418-X

Shekinah Publishers
394 Glory Road
Blountville, TN 37617

Acknowledgments

This book is the collaborative effort of many who are committed to its message and who offered their prayers, minds and hands to see the work accomplished. I want to gratefully thank the following people for their specific contributions.

Betsy Nelson: Thank you for the untold hours you gave laboring with me to disseminate the message of forgiveness, from being a forgiver yourself to working with me on all phases of the book—organizing the material, typing the drafts, rewriting, and serving as editor and critic. As Paul said of Stephanas, you have addicted yourself to this ministry. "For God is not unrighteous to forget your work and labor of love, which you have shown toward his name, in that you have ministered to the saints, and do minister" (Hebrews 6:10).

Sandra Hemera: For months of caring for the Nelson children and household that Betsy might devote her energies to this project.

Carol Noe: For your willingness to be drafted for the tedious task of coding the manuscript. I'm especially grateful for your prayers and concern for the Scriptural integrity of the book. Thanks so much for your help in "hammering out" the hard parts!

Julie Bland: For your words of encouragement and suggestions for clarity of expression.

Nick Adams: Nephew, thank you for applying your journalistic expertise to a careful reading of the manuscript. Your comments and suggestions were extremely valuable.

Glenna Adams: How fortunate for this author to have a professional proofreader as her sister! Many thanks for your help with this endeavor.

Jane Lambert: For the use of your artistic eye for the cover design and, as a co-laborer in the gospel, for faithfully walking with me through many of the experiences recounted in this book.

Judson Cornwall and David Schoch: My dear friends and fellow ministers who urged me to write on this subject—and pressed to see it done! Thank you for your expressions of confidence, encouragement and support.

Contents

Dedicated to the Holy Spirit, who has taught me all I know about forgiveness; and without whose comfort I could not have learned the often painful lessons.

Introduction

The subject of forgiveness has always been a dominant theological theme, but today it is receiving widespread treatment by secular philosophers and physicians. Society as a whole has realized the negative personal consequences of anger, bitterness, and resentment. It appears a sin-sick world is finally stumbling onto the kingdom key the church has held all along—or have we?

The message and mission of the church is forgiveness. It is the crux of the Gospel, and Christians have been made ministers of reconciliation to impart this good news of forgiveness to all mankind. But before the message of forgiveness can successfully be taken to "the uttermost parts of the earth" it must be heard "first in Jerusalem."

Our churches maintain their vitality through the cleansing and release of forgiveness. God's forgiveness of our sins as individuals is our entrance into life in His Kingdom. Likewise the flow of forgiveness within and from the church sustains our corporate life in God. The disease of unforgiveness threatens that life for *where the church fails to forgive it ceases to live.*

Jesus said there is a plenteous harvest for the church to reap but the laborers are few. One of the major reasons the laborers are few is the unhealed state of the church because of unforgiveness. We know that in Christ's work of redemption our sins are eternally forgiven through a vertical transaction between ourselves and the Lord, but believers have not realized the power of forgiveness that operates on a horizontal level. While we rejoice in God's eternal forgiveness of our sins through the blood of Jesus, our unforgiveness of one another forbids us to walk in the liberty He died to bring us.

This horizontal aspect is a major element of forgiveness that most of us Christians have never considered. With the secular world, we have sought to rid ourselves of the negative personal consequences of unforgiveness, but what impact does our collective unforgiveness have on the life and ministry of the church? What impression of God's Kingdom of righteousness, peace, and joy is the church giving the world?

We will experience seasons and situations which will greatly strain our ability to say from our hearts, "I forgive you." But if we entertain the enemy's subtle suggestion that we have the option *not to forgive*, we detour from our journey of being conformed to His image. If we are going to be effective as the Body of Christ in the earth, our understanding of forgiveness must *grow up*.

FOUNDATIONS OF THE FORGIVING CHURCH

Jesus laid a significant foundation of principles governing this horizontal dimension of forgiveness.

His teachings and declarations concerning forgiveness probe deeply into our responsibilities as Spirit-led Christians. We must enlarge our sphere of concern beyond our individual needs to obtain the love and unity necessary for the corporate health of the church.

If we are to mature as co-laborers with Christ we must be willing to pay the price of entering into the fellowship of His suffering. Jesus' heart attitude for dealing with the rejection of men was, "Father forgive them, they know not what they do." Forgiveness is the manifestation of the cross-life. Will we find an alternate pathway in keeping our hearts united with His Kingdom purpose?

The church has preached restoration. Now she is learning that the power of it is forgiveness. Jesus stated His mission in Luke 4:18, "to preach the gospel to the poor . . . to heal the broken-hearted, to preach deliverance to the captive and recovering of sight to the blind, to set at liberty them that are bruised." Our success in accomplishing any of these ministries is predicated upon our walking in forgiveness.

FUNCTIONING AS THE FORGIVING CHURCH

In His teachings on forgiveness Jesus not only tells us *why* we must forgive one another; He delineates *how* we are to walk with each other in forgiveness. It is as our lifestyles reflect our beliefs that the Kingdom of God comes to earth. The redemptive fellowship of the church becomes a place of refuge and peace.

Yet it is possible for the church to assent to the

foundation of forgiveness in word and fail to build upon it in deed and in truth.

The church's failure to forgive does not stem from refusals but from deceptions. We misunderstand the nature of forgiveness and fail to follow the Scriptural procedures for forgiving one another. Our surface relationships are hypocritical and reveal that we have neglected to examine our heart attitudes toward one another. If we are to function as a household of faith in Christ's image, the church must be delivered from a facade of forgiveness and experience the redemptive work Jesus died to bring us.

All Christians accept that forgiveness from God is a life and death matter for the individual. Now we must face the ramifications the question of forgiveness holds for the lives of our churches, and ultimately, for the ministry of God's Kingdom in the earth. How will we respond to the call to become the Forgiving Church?

Part I

Foundations of the Forgiving Church

1

Fact of Forgiveness

The kingdom of God is ... righteousness, peace, and joy in the Holy Ghost (Romans 14:17).

If our churches are to be demonstrations of God's kingdom in the earth they must bear these three hallmarks: righteousness, peace and joy. The foundation of all of these is forgiveness. Our righteousness before God is made through the forgiveness of sins by the blood of Jesus. The joy of our salvation also springs from the fact of forgiveness (Psalm 51:12). Then there is peace, that precious reality that the world so longs for; it too finds its underpinnings in forgiveness (Romans 5:1).

As one third of the kingdom reality, peace must characterize the lifestyle we share together as the church. Our personal peace with God has no expression if it is not shared with our brothers and sisters in the Body of Christ. We must walk in peace with one another or we are giving the world a false picture of God's kingdom. There is no peace apart from forgiveness. If we will reach out to lay hold on forgiveness for ourselves and our churches then truly the kingdom of God can come to earth.

FORGIVENESS: GOD'S PROVISION FOR PEACE

From Jesus' first appearance to His disciples after His resurrection we find understanding concerning the relationship between forgiveness and the manifestation of the peace of God's Kingdom.

> Then the same day at evening, being the first day of the week, when the doors were shut where the disciples were assembled for fear of the Jews, came Jesus and stood in the midst, and saith unto them, Peace be unto you. And when he had so said, he showed them his hands and his side (John 20:19-20).

Where did the peace He gave them come from? His hands and side. It came from His blood; it came from forgiveness. Jesus had just made the provision of forgiveness by presenting His blood at the throne of God.

He had previously appeared to Mary Magdalene and when she reached out to touch him, he said to her, "Touch me not; for I am not yet ascended to my Father" John 20:17). According to the law of Moses, once a year the high priest was to come before the presence of God to offer the blood of bulls and goats as an atonement for the sin of the people. If he was touched before he entered the Holy of Holies he would be defiled.

When Jesus had this conversation with Mary He was on His way to present His blood before the throne of God. Jesus, as our Great High Priest, "by his own blood, he entered in once into the holy place, having obtained eternal redemption for us" (Hebrews 9:12). The Father accepted the blood of His Son as the atonement for the sins of the whole world and said, "I forgive them!"

Because He had completed the transaction that secured their forgiveness, Jesus could now come to His followers and say, "Peace be unto you." He greeted them with His intention and plan for their lives: "For the kingdom of God is . . . righteousness, peace and joy in the Holy Ghost" (Romans 14:17). The blood of forgiveness is God's provision for our peace. There is no peace without the cross. Peace came through His wounds, from the shedding of His blood. Peace means reconciliation and it is through the cross that we are reconciled to God. *We have no peace apart from the place where peace has been made.*

The word of God speaks against the false prophets who cried, "Peace, peace; when there is no peace" (Jeremiah 6:14). I have heard people say, "We're just a happy church!" They're clapping their hands and "everything is going along fine" while the church grows to be four or five hundred—and then they have a split. "But we had wonderful peace," they claim. They grow again and then have three factions, and they're still clapping their hands saying, "But we have peace."

Once while driving down a country road I passed a church named Harmony. A few miles further down that same road I passed New Harmony Church, which meant there wasn't harmony in Harmony Church. I've even heard people say such ridiculous things as, "good wood splinters," meaning the church was so good it had to split. If another church needs to be started, then let a group be commissioned to go out peacefully. God does not build His kingdom of peace through war.

Why do churches have divisions, factions, turmoil, chaos? Why do they lack peace? *Unforgiveness.* Oh, we say, it must be more than that. We can't expect everyone in the church to always see things eye to eye. That is true, but in love we can find a place of resolving our differences of opinion. The basis of unresolved difficulties in the church is still unforgiveness.

FORGIVENESS: THE COMMISSION OF THE CHURCH

Unless we tap into God's power to become the Forgiving Church we'll never have peace. Jesus' first address to the disciples after the resurrection shows us how to enter into this forgiving power. Jesus began His discourse with a declaration of peace. He ended it with a profound statement about the forgiveness of sins.

> "Whosoever's sins you remit, they are remitted unto them; and whosoever's sins you retain they are retained" (John 20:23).

This scripture presents Christians with a startling challenge concerning forgiveness. The New International Version states this concept even more directly: "If you forgive anyone his sins, they are forgiven, and if you do not forgive them they are not forgiven." Jesus has said something positively radical to His disciples. Looking at this verse I began to consider, what if this really means what it says?

Now, please relax. I'm not building a doctrinal or theological treatise. I don't pretend to know all that this verse means. I just want us to consider together, what if this were true? Just the way Jesus says it.

Think about it for a moment and be paralyzed! If you forgive anyone his sins, they are forgiven, and if you do not forgive them they are not forgiven. Can that possibly mean what it says? We do know that it does mean what it *means*! What is the significance of this verse in relation to forgiveness?

We understand that no person can keep another from receiving forgiveness from God. The unforgiveness that men may hold against us in no way interferes with our justification before God through the blood of Jesus. If we repent, He is faithful and just to forgive us (1 John 1:9). Conversely, another person's forgiveness of our sins cannot negotiate our salvation with God. Whatever implications this verse may have concerning the role of Christians in relation to forgiving people's sins, we know that the eternal aspect of forgiveness is totally under God's control.

If Jesus' statement is not dealing with the forgiveness of sins in an eternal sense, then the church must be involved in another dimension in which forgiveness—and the withholding of it—operates. The preceding verses put Jesus' words into context for us. His declaration concerning forgiving sins is a part of His first directives to the infant church. In verse 21 He says, "As my Father hath sent me, even so send I you." Here Jesus is commissioning them *as His church* to continue the work He had begun in bringing the Kingdom of God to earth.

What Jesus then said and did provides the key to our understanding the significance of this entire passage: "And, when He had said this, He breathed on them and said unto them, 'Receive ye the Holy Ghost' " (v. 22). It was *after* Jesus had spoken these words and breathed on them that He made His declaration about forgiving sins.

When God breathes the Holy Spirit upon us, upon our churches, He breathes His life into us and we begin to operate in a dimension of power in God's Spirit. He allows us to taste of the world to come as we move into heavenly realms with Jesus in praying and believing. At the same time God invests us with a greater level of responsibility in forgiving one another.

At the time Jesus spoke these words to His disciples He had just completed the transaction with the Father that sealed the forgiveness necessary for our salvation. He appointed His followers to carry this message of reconciliation to the world. He then gave us the power by the Holy Spirit, and the authority by His declaration on forgiveness, to be the forgiving church.

"As my Father hath sent me, even so send I you." The church finds the nature of her commission detailed in John 3:17, "For God sent not his Son into the world to condemn the world; but that the world through him might be saved." We have been given the message of salvation, of forgiveness of sins. Through the Holy Spirit our message has the power to liberate the hearts and minds of all who desire forgiveness. This good news of the gospel does not end with the initial salvation experience. The forgiving church continually experiences redemption through the blood of Jesus and the forgiveness of sins.

If the Spirit-baptized church has been given the authority to minister blessing through forgiveness, what effect does our unforgiveness have on people?

Beyond denying people the comfort of love and acceptance, the unforgiveness of those who are filled with the Holy Spirit can inhibit their experience of the liberty that Jesus died for them to have. When we as believers fail in our responsibility to forgive, our disagreements and negative opinions become tools of the enemy.

As a pastor I have observed the extent to which the unforgiveness of spirit-baptized believers can hurt a fellow Christian. At one time a small group in our church was particularly fervent in devotion to the Lord and spent much time in prayer and Bible study. In their desire for more knowledge and experience of God they became involved with mature Christians from another city.

At first these people were simply encouraging the members of our church, offering study materials and teaching them about prayer. But after a time certain doctrinal differences began to surface and they seemed to choose one member of our ministry staff as the focal point of their disagreement. They did not approve of this person's "approach to life" and judged him unfit for the ministry. Their influence over our members had become such that they agreed in prayer together that God would remove this minister from our church!

I was astounded at the effect their unforgiving, censorious judgment had on this person's life. The oppression robbed him of self-confidence and he was no longer able to minister with the God-given liberty he once had. He became depressed and even experienced inexplicable physical problems during this period. In fact, he became so discouraged that he considered leaving his place of ministry. In the end God removed the errant ones from our church rather

than the person they were praying against. He recovered from the ordeal and continues to minister
under God's anointing. But for that period of time
the unforgiving judgments of spirit-baptized believers
produced a very real bondage in his life.

In receiving the Holy Spirit, we enter into a spiritual realm that carries with it a power and a *responsibility* to forgive. When we exercise this power
according to our carnal judgments we oppose God's
decree of forgiveness and redemption. If we are not
going to operate as forgiving churches, then we
should not receive the Holy Spirit! Our unforgiveness
will undermine God's purpose for His church as a
redemptive fellowship.

FORGIVENESS: THE KINGDOM CALLING

In commissioning His followers to live as the Forgiving Church, Jesus established His provision for
peace on the earth. "Peace be with you; as the
Father is sending Me, I am sending you." Peace had
come because Jesus had shed His blood so that we
could be forgiven. Again Jesus said, "Peace be unto
you" and then He immediately gave them instruction
in how to have it: Here is the Holy Ghost. Now forgive each other.

Jesus' commission to His church is founded upon
the *fact of forgiveness*. We are called as the Body of
Christ in the earth to demonstrate His forgiveness
of sins. Let's stop forgiving ourselves for walking in
unforgiveness that we may live in the peace that
Jesus shed His blood for us to have. If a church
wants to do something beautiful for God, every
member must make the decision to live and walk in
forgiveness, no matter what the cost.

2

Force of Forgiveness

Whatever you bind on earth will be bound in heaven
and whatever you loose on earth will be loosed in heaven
(Matthew 18:18).

Jesus initially revealed to Peter the power of the
church to bind and loose, stating that He would give
him the keys of the kingdom to activate this power.

And I will give unto thee the keys of the kingdom of
heaven: and whatsoever thou shalt bind on earth shall
be bound in heaven: and whatsoever thou shalt loose
on earth shall be loosed in heaven (Matthew 16:19).

Jesus identifies one of these kingdom keys for us
when He makes this declaration again in Matthew
18:18. This declaration concerning binding and loosing is right in the middle of Jesus' teaching on the
dynamics of forgiveness. From its context in this
passage we can conclude that the understanding and
exercise of forgiveness is a Kingdom Key relating to
the power of binding and loosing.

Jesus depicts the power of loosing as the force of
forgiveness in a parable in verses 23-25. A man owed
a debt so great that his master had given command

for the man and his family to be sold as slaves. Because the man worshiped him and begged for his patience, his master "was moved with compassion and loosed him, and forgave him the debt" (v. 27). The man who needed to be forgiven a great debt was *loosed* from it.

This Greek word translated loose is *apoluo* which means to release, dismiss or set at liberty. This same root word and its concept is found in Luke 4:18 where Jesus states that He is anointed for the purpose of "setting at liberty them that are bruised." We have often thought that loosing had to do with prayers of deliverance or healing. Or perhaps we were expecting some miraculous intervention of the Holy Spirit. But Matthew 18 teaches us that through forgiveness we actually release a power that looses men from their bruisings. When the kingdom key of forgiveness is turned, the door of liberty is unlocked and the captive can be set free.

THE POWER TO BIND AND LOOSE

This power of loosing is one of the greatest aspects of the ministry of forgiveness. We can loose God's Spirit to deliver and set the captive free. However, if our forgiveness of one another has the power to loose, it must also be true that our unforgiveness *binds*. The power of forgiveness to bind or loose should not surprise us. It is Jesus' forgiveness toward us that has loosed us from the penalty and power of unforgiven sin that had bound our own lives. The teaching Jesus brought to His disciples was that through withholding or releasing forgiveness they also entered into a dimension of binding and loosing.

Jesus speaks of these contrasting effects in Matthew 18:18, "Whatever you bind on earth will be bound in heaven and whatever you loose on earth will be loosed in heaven."

Most Christians are familiar with this scripture. It has been a favorite among those who desire to exercise authority over satan in order to see God's will accomplished. But the power of the verse has not been properly understood because it has been taken out of context and stood alone as a command, "Satan, I bind you." Actually this verse is a part of Jesus' teaching on the effects of forgiveness within the church. Immediately preceding this verse on binding and loosing, Jesus stresses the necessity of forgiving a brother who has sinned against us. He carefully outlines the steps to take, from going to the brother alone, to taking one or two more with us, and finally to the point of making it a church issue (Matthew 18:15-17). Diligence and the effort of persuasion are suggested in these instructions. Jesus is pressing the need for reconciliation.

He follows this commentary on forgiveness by saying, "Whatsoever ye bind on earth will be bound in heaven." In this context concerning forgiveness His words constitute a warning: If we do not forgive our brothers and sisters, *there will be a bondage in the church.* If we do not work at persuading them to be reconciled to us, we are allowing unforgiveness to bind the church from complete freedom in the heavenly realm. Whatever is bound on earth is bound in heaven. But when we loose a brother through forgiveness, that blessing is not only communicated to him on the earth; there is a commensurate spiritual loosing in heaven.

THE POWER OF AGREEMENT

The church is on the earth, but its power reaches into the heavenly realms where the forces of satan are continually working to resist the will of God. Jesus connects the force of forgiveness with the church's ability to overcome this resistance of the enemy in the verse following His instructions on binding and loosing, "Again I say unto you, that if two of you shall *agree* on earth as touching anything that they shall ask it shall be done for them of My Father which is in heaven" (Matthew 18:19).

Our power against the devil is in the agreement that we have when we are walking in forgiveness with one another. There is no need to say, "Devil, I bind you" when at the same time we are binding our brothers! We're always trying to bind the devil by binding the devil, but in fact we've loosed the devil when we bind our brothers through unforgiveness. Some have exhausted both spiritual and emotional energies endeavoring to bind the devil. We all want to see his power bound. The reality of this passage of scripture is that *when we loose our brother we bind the devil, and when we bind our brother we loose the devil.*

"If two of you shall agree on earth as touching anything that they shall ask it shall be done for them of My Father which is in heaven." "Agree with me that I'll get a new cadillac!" That's not what this verse is about. Jesus is speaking of the power of agreement that is released through the force of forgiveness. He speaks first about the loss of power through unforgiveness or irreconciliation. Our refusal to be reconciled binds our brothers and sisters, thereby binding the power of the church. But when we loose them, we loose the blessing of God in the congregation. If we are in harmony through reconciliation—if we will agree—He will be in our midst, "For where two or three are gathered in my name, there am I in the midst of them" (v. 20).

This understanding of our responsibility to forgive one another has an enormous impact on the lives of our churches. How we deal with one another directly affects our collective power in God's Kingdom. In 1980 the Lord visited the church at Shekinah in Holy Ghost revival. The power of God's Spirit was manifestly present among us for a number of months as the whole church prayed together every morning and evening. Many of the truths that He revealed to us during this time directly concerned forgiveness. He showed us that the primary requirement for the Holy Spirit to be present among a people was that they be continually reconciled to one another. If there was anything wrong among us we were to make it right quickly.

During this time we came to expect an intense visitation of the Spirit each time we met together. If we came to pray and noticed a cold, dead stillness, we would all sit and say, "Lord, is it I?" Then the Holy Spirit would speak to one or more of us. Perhaps we needed to confess something to the whole group or maybe to go privately to an individual; at times the resolution was effected just between ourselves and the Lord. After we obeyed the Holy Spirit's prompting we would experience a greater manifestation of His presence. Our experience confirmed to us that we do place certain restrictions on the moving of God's Spirit throughout the Body of Christ through our unforgiveness. We walked in this reality and understood that God absolutely requires that there be no unforgiveness among us. I personally did not hear a single word of backbiting among our people from 1980 to 1984. Further, we saw that through our withholding or releasing of forgiveness we could either bind or loose His presence to move on our hearts—and the hearts of others.

Individuals in the same church who harbor unforgiving thoughts and attitudes toward each other bind the efforts of the congregation. As they endeavor to pray together in the same prayer meeting, the bondage created by their unforgiveness robs that prayer meeting of the liberty of the Holy Ghost as well as the power of agreement to have their prayers answered. This bondage of unforgiveness also operates among churches and pastors who should be joining their prayer power in order to bring down strongholds in their city or nation. Only as all of us function as the *Forgiving Church* will we have the liberty to see God's purposes fully accomplished in the earth.

RELEASING THE POWER

We must make every effort for reconciliation with the members of the body of Christ, following the steps Jesus outlined in Matthew 18. But what about those who refuse to be reconciled? Obviously, after we have made every effort, the situation is out of our hands. But the fact that a person refuses to be reconciled to us cannot affect our forgiveness toward him. *The goal is reconciliation but the command is forgiveness.*

Some Christians require people to repent before they will forgive them. A true understanding of the power of loosing dispels this misconception. The Greek word *apolou* that is translated to loose or to forgive also carries the understanding "I stand back from a thing." The fact that a person has not repented does not give us a right to bind him in unforgiveness. Our attitude must be "I stand back from endeavoring to bind you. I refuse to bind you in my unforgiveness. I loose you from negative, critical and judgmental attitudes." Our forgiveness of people is not predicated on their repentance but rather on our willingness to release them from our judgments against them.

It is hypocritical to wait for people to repent and then say, "Now that he's repented, I feel okay toward him again." That is not forgiveness; that's agreement with the person's repentance! Forgiveness is freeing the transgressor, the one who is treating us badly. We loose him from any negative attitudes and we pray for the revelation of truth to come to him. "I forgive you." What a power there is in those words! If we want to release people from the bondage of sin, we must *first* release them from the bondage of our unforgiveness. When the force of forgiveness is loosed the heavens are opened for the power of God's Spirit to deal with the hearts of men.

If a person does not desire to be reconciled, we can hold our forgiveness in our hearts on deposit until he comes to collect it. That is what Jesus did for us. If anyone comes to Jesus and receives the work and power of His blood in what He did on Calvary, forgiveness is his. It is on deposit waiting for anyone to come and collect it. God's Word teaches that we have a part in ministering His forgiveness to others. "God was in Christ, reconciling the world to himself, not imputing their trespasses and sins unto them; *and hath committed to us the word of reconciliation*" (2 Corinthians 5:19). When we are sinned against, we can immediately choose to forgive. If our forgiveness is not accepted, we can hold it in our heart until it is collected. If it is never collected, our peace will return to us (Matthew 10:13).

Our forgiveness will not always effect reconciliation, but a state of irreconciliation must not alter our attitude of forgiveness toward our brother. Forgiveness opens the door for reconciliation. Our continuing in forgiveness preserves the possibility, though that reconciliation may be years in coming. I have personally experienced the long term effects of the power of loosing through forgiveness.

In the early years of our work there was a woman in our church whom I loved and appreciated. She was very supportive, helpful in prayer and ministry, and committed to the vision God had put in my heart. As the work developed there were some areas in which she disagreed and eventually she and her family chose to leave the church. Charged with negative feelings, the parting was very painful to both of us.

Being young in the things of God, I thought that He would have her return and ask my forgiveness for not seeing things my way. To my surprise, a few months after she left the Lord told me to go and ask *her* forgiveness for any way in which I had hurt her when she left. I obeyed His instructions and she accepted my apology, but there was no reconciliation at that point. From that time I retained the posture of forgiveness, "I loose you from any negative thoughts that I might have and I pray the blessing of God to be your portion."

Several years passed and I received a phone call from her saying that she wanted me to know that she loved me and was praying for me. She said that she was sorry for the negative experiences that had passed between us. Though the work was not complete, she had taken a step toward reconciliation.

A few years later she called to ask if we could get together in a city where I was going to minister. She came to hear me preach twice that Sunday. Both messages were requested by the host pastor. The subject was forgiveness! Afterwards I invited her to visit with me in the home of my host and we talked for several hours. Finally she, being a straightforward person, said, "What do you want from me?" I said, "Come back into my heart and let it be as if all these negative things had never happened." She also desired that all differences be set aside through forgiveness. We were truly reconciled to one another; our relationship was restored. How long did it take? Eleven years. But when it happened it was real and the strife was over—really over!

Loose your brother through the force of forgiveness. Give him a space of blessing in which to respond. Place him in God's hands by releasing him from your grip.

In chapter 7 of the book of Acts a man named Stephen was unjustly stoned at the hands of self-righteous men. As he was dying, Stephen looked up into heaven and said, "Lay not this sin to their charge" (v. 60). As they were killing him, he was forgiving them. Maybe a Sunday school teacher once told you that was sweet of him. That wasn't sweet, that was *power*!

Who was affected by the power of that forgiveness?

The very next verse says that Paul (then called Saul) stood there giving approval to Stephen's death. He even held the garments of those who martyred Stephen. The man who took the gospel to the Gentiles and penned a major part of the New Testament was forgiven by Stephen before he was saved. Is it possible that when Stephen mouthed these words of forgiveness he loosed Paul to believe?

The force of forgiveness brings a loosing that makes a way for God to work. As churches we must come to the place of immediately ministering forgiveness to one another—in every situation. Our forgiveness is so much more than a choice of whether our pride can "handle this one." Our forgiveness rattles the very gates of hell and comes before the throne of God to make a way for people to repent and believe.

3

First Forgiveness

Shouldest not thou also have had compassion on thy fellowservant, even as I had pity on thee? (Matthew 18:33)

After Jesus revealed to His disciples the unlimited power that was available to them in loosing each other through forgiveness, Peter asked Him a very telling question, "Lord, how oft shall my brother sin against me, and I forgive him? till seven times?" (Matthew 18:21). Our human nature acts as though forgiveness were a judgment of God upon us rather than the administration of His peace. Instead of rejoicing in the wonderful force of forgiveness, the disciples revealed the stinginess of their hearts in looking for a place where they could stop forgiving!

Forgiveness does not have a stopping point. Jesus' answer to Peter was not seven times but seventy times seven! (v. 22) His answer revealed the difference between a church that forgives—to a point, and a forgiving church. When pressed to forgive we often find ourselves like Peter, asking the wrong question. We will not find the motivation to forgive by asking

"How much must we forgive?" The issue of forgiveness will be settled in our hearts when we know *"Why must we forgive?"* After exposing the fault of Peter's question, Jesus told His disciples a story that gave the answer to the question they should have asked.

THE PRECEDENT OF FORGIVENESS

> Therefore is the kingdom of heaven likened unto a certain king, which would take account of his servants. And when he had begun to reckon, one was brought unto him, which owed him ten thousand talents. But forasmuch as he had not to pay, his lord commanded him to be sold, and his wife, and children, and all that he had, and payment to be made. The servant therefore fell down, and worshipped him, saying, Lord, have patience with me, and I will pay thee all. Then the lord of that servant was moved with compassion, and loosed him, and forgave him the debt (Matthew 18:23-27).

One translation says that the servant owed his master sixty million dollars—an amount that he couldn't possibly repay. We all stand in the place of that master's servant: through the blood of Jesus we have been forgiven our insurmountable debt of sin. Forgiveness of sins is the crux of the gospel message; it is the good news to a world of people who owe debts they can never repay.

So why should we forgive one another? Because other people say that we should or because the preacher has made us feel guilty when we didn't? We are the sixty million dollar debtors. Jesus forgave us an insurmountable debt. If Jesus had not died for us we would not be forgiven. Though we are the ones that deserved hell, our sins have all been washed away by the precious blood of Jesus. *The fact that we have been forgiven a great debt is the central motivation for us to forgive others.*

This *first* forgiveness that Jesus made in shedding His blood on the cross accomplished more than personal salvation. Beyond rendering us acceptable to God as individuals, the work of redemption instituted a whole new order for relationships among God's people. The "eye for an eye" of the Old Testament law became the "love your enemies" of the Sermon on the Mount. In that teaching in Matthew 5 Jesus was not expounding an ivory-towered ideal; He was describing the way of life in His kingdom!

All of our transactions with one another in the church are based on the first forgiveness. We forgive because we are forgiven. Forgiveness is the manner of God's kingdom. Then what sort of picture of the kingdom does our *unforgiveness* paint? Jesus continues His story.

THE PERVERSION OF UNFORGIVENESS

But the same servant went out, and found one of his fellowservants, which owed him an hundred pence: and he laid hands on him, and took him by the throat, saying, Pay me that thou owest. And his fellowservant fell down at his feet, and besought him, saying, Have patience with me and I will pay thee all. And he would not: but went and cast him into prison, till he should pay the debt (Matthew 18:28-30).

How do we respond to those who sin against us? We often find ourselves in the shoes of the unmerciful servant. Compared to the sixty million dollar debt, his fellow servant owed him sixteen dollars. The scripture says that "he took him by the throat." Perhaps we should examine the throats of our brothers and sisters to see if they bear our fingerprints! Unforgiveness chokes the Body of Christ.

We seldom realize the impact our unforgiveness has on the life of the church. We may come to a church meeting and find the worship dull or we may wonder why so few appear ministered to by the preaching. We don't realize that the negative atmosphere created by collective unforgiveness stifles the moving of the Holy Spirit among us. Our assemblies can be bound by the very ones who say they have come to receive from the Lord.

After the man who had been forgiven the great debt had taken his fellow servant by the throat, he cast him into prison until he could repay him. The irony is that it is impossible for a person to repay a debt when he is in prison. In harboring unforgiveness we put people into absolutely impossible situations. They are helpless to resolve the problems they may have caused and the resulting disunity hinders the effectiveness of the whole church.

Often in our unforgiveness we put people in prison for life for a sixteen dollar debt. What little thing has someone done to you that you haven't yet forgiven them for? Put a little scratch on your car? And they never got it fixed! Mine has four such places—my poor car, wounded in the house of my friends. I don't have a right to remember any of those incidences with a negative thought. Why? Because it was a "sixteen dollar debt." Our response is often, "They should have fixed it!" Well, they didn't.

Are we going to live our lives in the "should haves" or in reality?

It is strange how we comfort one another in our unforgiveness. We cry to each other about how we just can't seem to forgive someone and then take solace when our confidante agrees with us and tells us that they wouldn't be able to forgive such a thing either, as if his opinion validates our unforgiveness! We nurse our wounds and replay the memory videos of all our hurts and recount who did each thing to us. We console one another and consent together that our offenders should not be forgiven. But the Father does not agree with our excuses. His pronouncement on our unforgiveness is that of the master in the parable. When he found that his servant refused to forgive, he said to him, "O, thou wicked servant, I forgave thee all that debt, because thou desiredst me: Shouldest not thou also have had compassion on thy fellowservant, even as I had pity on thee?" (Matthew 18:32-33).

Wicked is derived from the same Old English word as *wicker*, as in wicker furniture. In the process of making wicker, a certain type of plant stem is bent or twisted into the desired form. The scriptural reference to the "wicked servant" could be more explicitly rendered *twisted* or *perverse* servant. Saved people who refuse to forgive are twisted. They are perverting the gospel that says, "I forgave thee all that debt." When we have been forgiven so much and refuse to forgive the small, trifling things others do to us, Jesus calls this perverse. That is what this whole story is about. Unforgiveness is a perversion. It is intolerable in a people that have been forgiven.

THE PRICE OF UNFORGIVENESS

And his lord was wroth and delivered him to the tormentors till he should pay all that was due unto him. So likewise shall my heavenly Father do also unto you, if ye from your hearts forgive not every one his brother their trespasses (vv. 33-34).

No one goes free when there is unforgiveness. One was in prison and the other one was delivered over to the tormentors. Jesus said the same torment will follow every Christian who refuses to forgive his brothers. How many people are born again but are plagued by the tormentors of their own guilt and unforgiveness? Every day their tormentors come to collect from them. A daily toll is taken on our lives when in mind and emotion we don't release others as God has released us. We wake up each morning under the weight of oppression. We end up in a bondage of thoughts, fears and inferiorities of our own making and don't understand how this has come to pass.

Once after I had ministered on forgiveness a woman approached me and said, "I can never get these things resolved in my life because my father was an alcoholic." I replied, "I'm glad to meet you; so was mine." It is our unforgiveness that perpetuates the suffering of past painful situations. Torments come to us because of unforgiveness—tormentors of guilt, fear, dread, hatred, even of physical problems. The tragedy is that we resist the truth and never experience the relief brought by simply forgiving.

THE PROVISION OF FORGIVENESS

God doesn't call us to unconditional forgiveness because He is not aware of what has been done to us. He created forgiveness to release us from the torment of injustices, negative emotions, hurtful relationships, resentment, and even the torment of our own personalities. His plan isn't for us to just keep hanging on and someday go to heaven. He intends for us to be free in mind and spirit while we still dwell on this earth.

Jesus has made a wonderful provision for the negative things that are going to happen to us along the way. It is called forgiveness. We appropriate this provision by understanding what transpired in Jesus' heart at the first forgiveness on Calvary. No one was more sinned against than Jesus, but when He hung on the cross He declared, "Father, forgive them; for they know not what they do." We need the revelation of the heart of Jesus that says, "When people sin against us, they don't know what they are doing."

We say, "But they *do* know; they know *exactly* what they are doing. They are fully aware that they are hurting me." But the attitude of Jesus' heart is not based on what "they are doing." It springs from a pitiful compassion that sees people's need for redemption above the extent of their sin. We can draw from the heart of Jesus a love that swallows up their hate. "And above all things have fervent charity among yourselves: for charity shall cover the multitude of sins" (1 Peter 4:8). When we identify with the heart of Jesus in that first forgiveness, we can say of those who sin against us, "Father, forgive them. If they knew You as I know You they wouldn't be doing this. If they knew Your Calvary love as You have put it in my heart, they wouldn't be this blind."

The church cannot afford the price of unforgiveness. It is too high. If Christians keep one another in the cruel prison of unforgiveness and themselves in the torment of it, who will reap the harvest? Who will preach the gospel, who will bind up the brokenhearted, and set the captives free? Why don't we just let *everyone* out of prison. We can as we yield to the expectation of the first forgiveness: "I cancelled all that debt of yours ... Shouldn't you have mercy on your fellowservant just as I had mercy on you?"

4

Furnace of Forgiveness

> Beloved, think it not strange concerning the fiery
> trial which is to try you, as though some strange
> thing happened unto you: But rejoice, inasmuch as
> ye are partakers of Christ's sufferings; that, when
> his glory shall be revealed, ye may be glad with
> exceeding joy (1 Peter 4:12-13).

The work of forgiveness is a furnace; *it is meant
to be*. It is part of the fiery trial Peter speaks of in
the above passage, "Beloved, think it not strange,"
but we do think it strange! We have a cringing fear
and dread of anything that is painful. More lies are
told with hymnals in our hands than perhaps any
other way. We solemnly sing, "I surrender all," or
"Where He leads me I will follow." But when He
leads us into the crucible of life where we are tried
relating to our love for those around us, we balk.

We have rejoiced and prayed upon the promises of
God—those for healing, deliverance and prosperity.
But when we are persecuted or betrayed, we fear
we must be out of His will, or that He is displeased
with us. But He promised us betrayal (Mark 13:12).

He promised us persecution (2 Tim. 3:12). We have desired a Christianity without a cross. We cannot enjoy the promises of blessing apart from the circumstances that pierce our hearts. The furnace of forgiveness provides the opportunity for us to be conformed to the image of Christ in the midst of our trials.

GLORY IN THE FURNACE

For our light affliction, which is for but a moment, worketh for us a far more exceeding and eternal weight of glory (2 Corinthians 4:17).

Finding the Fourth Man

The literal furnace experience of Shadrach, Meshach, and Abednego related in Daniel chapter 3 gives us a vivid picture of this glory. Though the fire consumed those who threw them into it, the furnace served only to loose the bonds of the three Hebrew children. They emerged from the ordeal without even the smell of smoke upon them. Not only were they preserved; they found release in the midst of the burning. Why? Those looking on saw "four men ... walking in the midst of the fire ... the form of the fourth ... like the Son of God" (v. 25). They were not alone in their trial. Because there was a Fourth Man in the furnace with them, the fire had only glorious effects upon them. It is not the difficulties and pressure we endure that will change us; it is finding the Fourth Man in the flames.

We haven't experienced the power of His presence if Jesus hasn't made us more like Himself in the course of what we have been through. If our furnace is only a place of misery and discomfort, then we suffer in vain. When we come through our betrayals and disappointments bearing bitterness and negative attitudes, the smell of smoke is upon us. It is meeting the Fourth Man in the fire that preserves us from debilitating injury and scars. The understanding He brings us in our trials delivers us from every power the fire has to harm us.

If we yield to the way of forgiveness and trust in His grace, Jesus can minister to our pain and bewilderment. Then the furnace becomes a place of purification to conform us to His own image. The revelation of the Fourth Man in the furnace will transform our lives.

Aligning Our Character

In the Sermon on the Mount in Matthew 5, Jesus furnishes us with the foundational understanding of the furnace work of forgiveness. He begins in verse 39 by saying, "Whosoever shall smite thee on thy right cheek, turn to him the other also." This verse is followed by a volley of similar instructions.

> And if any man will sue thee at the law, and take away thy coat, let him have thy cloak also. And whosoever shall compel thee to go a mile with him, go with him twain. . . . Love your enemies, bless them that curse you, do good to them that hate you, and pray for them which despitefully use you and persecute you (vv. 40, 41, 44).

The next verse gives the reason for His instructions: "That ye may be the children of your Father which is in heaven." What is Jesus asking for here? *A character alignment with the Father.* Parents want the children they have begotten to look like them. And that is the Father's desire for us. Is there enough evidence in our lives to show who our Father is? By turning the other cheek and going the second mile we demonstrate the unconditional love of our heavenly Father. When we feel that we are having to forgive more than others do, we can be comforted in knowing that God is entrusting us with more opportunity to be conformed to the image of His Son. Jesus also "learned obedience through the things that He suffered" (Hebrews 5:8).

GIVING IN THE FURNACE

"Give me your coat."

"Alright. By all means take my cloak also."

"Go with me one mile."

"Certainly, I'll go with you two."

"You're hitting me on my right cheek? Here, try the other one."

Our human nature is extremely opposed to the furnace of forgiveness. We are more likely to hide our cheek in our collar before someone can hit the first one! Our natural response to the call to forgive is, "It's not fair!" That's right. It's not fairness . . . it is forgiveness.

Have people ever taken something from you? Then you prayed a "God-get-em" prayer and they returned everything and apologized, right? We all know from experience that almost never happens. Until we are willing to give up, yield up, turn our backs on what we would have had if they hadn't taken it from us, we will not be able to forgive.

A man once came to me with a situation that was giving him great difficulty. He said, "Because of the financial problems my wife had before we were married, I am now having to do without some things." I told him, "If you forgive you must accept the fact that you will suffer some loss."

We have not understood that in forgiveness *someone always loses*. Forgive is from the Old English word forthgive. Forgiving means to "give forth." Sometimes it will mean giving up; sometimes it will mean giving in; but it will always mean giving. Giving is the crux of Christianity: God so loved the world that He gave. It is a simple fact that wherever there is a giver there is going to be a taker.

If we learn that the answer to takers is to give, we will never resent. *Resentment comes when we gave more than we meant to and when someone took more than we were ready to give.* If we are willing to give what is required of us and are prepared at all times to give above what we had planned to, we will never be plagued with resentment. If people take our reputation, let them have it. If they take our money, let them have it. There is power in godly surrender.

GLADNESS IN THE FURNACE

On the cross Jesus proved forgiveness as God's power to deliver wicked men. He has not asked us to suffer what He has not already experienced. He has felt the "feeling of our infirmities" in forgiving wicked men and knows that forgiveness is painful. He is fully aware of the depth of man's iniquity. It is *because* men are evil that there must be a way beyond getting even or striking a bargain.

This is the realm of understanding into which Paul had entered when he said, "for whom I have suffered the loss of all things, and do count them but dung, that I may win Christ ... That I may know him, and the power of his resurrection, and the *fellowship of his sufferings*, being made conformable to his death." (Philippians 3:8, 10). We enter into a special fellowship with Jesus when we are willing to suffer as He did, the just for the unjust.

If we yield ourselves to the furnace of forgiveness we *will* lose some things. What did Jesus forfeit when He paid the price to forgive us? God took on Himself the form of a man, and even less than a man, a slave. Jesus divested Himself of His glory, "He humbled Himself, and became obedient unto death, even the death of the cross" (Philippians 2:8).

In forgiveness we prepare the way for another to win. Even if we have to lose. But no matter what price we pay in our forgiving of others, God will make up our loss. What did He do to make up for Jesus' loss? "Wherefore God also hath highly exalted him, and given him a name above every name" (v. 9). It is the same with us. If we will be obedient even to the "death" of forgiveness God will bring exaltation: "Humble yourselves therefore under the mighty hand of God, that he may exalt you in due time" (2 Peter 5:6).

"But rejoice, inasmuch as ye are partakers of Christ's sufferings; that, when his glory shall be revealed, ye may be glad with exceeding joy."

5

Face of Forgiveness

> Neither do I condemn thee: go, and sin no more
> (John 8:11).

> But when he was yet a great way off, his father saw
> him, and had compassion, and ran, and fell on his
> neck, and kissed him (Luke 15:20).

Our brothers and sisters in the church will draw
upon our need to forgive in two different dimensions.
At times we must forgive people for violating God's
law even though they have not sinned against us
directly. Our temptation is to judge and label such
people and through unforgiveness to confine them in
the prison of our opinions. We will encounter other
situations in which people will sin against us personally. We must deal with the pain and possibly
the loss their behavior brings to our lives. Both of
these demands for forgiveness will try our willingness to respond according to Jesus' teachings.

What does forgiveness look like? Can someone
draw us a picture that we may see the beauty of
the forgiving heart? Is there a way to bring forth a

portrait of the wonderful work of forgiveness that God has given to us through Jesus Christ?

God's Word gives us more than principles of forgiveness to bring understanding to our minds. The life and parables of Jesus give us many portraits of the face of forgiveness that our hearts might be united with the Father's.

Of these portraits, two particularly depict the forgiving heart of God. They are the compassionate face of mercy for one who had transgressed the law, and the joyful face of benevolence for one whose behavior had brought pain and loss. Darkening the background of both of these portraits of forgiveness are the shadowy forms of those who oppose the forgiving face: the cold, hard visage of the religious legalist and the disapproving frown of the self-righteous.

JESUS, THE PHARISEES AND THE WOMAN

The scene is ancient Jerusalem. Jewish Pharisees have just caught a woman in adultery, in the very act. What an uproar—the surprise, the struggle, the shouting! The woman is dragged from the house to the noise of the swelling crowd surging down the street, "Take her to Jesus! Let's see how Jesus will judge her." (Whenever I read this passage of scripture I always wonder what happened to the man. And how did those "righteous" Pharisees know this woman's address?)

Finding Jesus, they thrust the woman before Him. What an ill-cast melodrama: the villain, a silent, bewildered woman; the heroes, a posse of agitated men clamoring for her blood. They demand a judgment from Jesus; "This woman was caught in the very act of adultery. The law of Moses commands us to stone such women. What do you say?"

The Pharisees do not care about the fate of this woman. She is merely bait in the trap they are setting for Jesus. They seek grounds to publicly accuse Him of undermining the law of God. Their hard faces match their hard hearts—hearts of stone that value preserving doctrine more than preserving life.

Like these Pharisees many "law-abiding" church members have a very religious answer for people who sin: kill them. And truly the law provides but one answer: kill the sinner. Whenever we choose to forgive there will always be those standing by accusing us of compromise. We must be convinced of what God's Word teaches about forgiveness, for there will always be those who are not willing to let people go free.

In their self-righteous frenzy the Pharisees have caught, accused, and sentenced. How long would it take us to build a church if we kept killing the sinners? Perhaps this is why some churches never grow. God brings people into the church through forgiveness. Forgiveness is also His plan for keeping them there.

All of us at some time wear the face of the Pharisee. We carefully focus our binoculars to view the faults of others. But when examining ourselves we look through the opposite end. Then we say with self-satisfaction "I am so fair-I-see." (Maybe that's where the word phar-i-see originated.)

But Jesus looks on the woman with eyes of compassion. His vision magnifies her need, not her sin. His response to what He sees is the Gospel, the commission to bring liberty to the captives, to set the prisoners free. Everything about the Gospel is good

news. What are we preaching to the people who
come to our churches broken and bruised by sin? If
it isn't good news it isn't the Gospel.

The Pharisees press in with their eyes narrowed,
their faces tense. They want action. "We demand a
judgment. Jesus, we want an answer now!" Sometimes we nice church people get worked up into a
froth about how holy we are and ask God, "What
are you going to do about all these other people who
aren't doing right?" When we find out what He's going to do with them, we're not going to like it as
much as we thought.

Jesus does not even answer the Pharisees. It appears He is pretending not to hear them. How the
contained face of forgiveness frustrates the contorted
one of unforgiveness. He calmly bends down to the
ground and begins to write with His finger in the
dust.

What is Jesus writing in the dust? Maybe He is
writing their sins. Or perhaps, "Go find out what
the scripture means that says 'I'll have mercy and
not sacrifice.'" We love to sacrifice by coming to
church, praying, and giving our offering, but it is
time we learned about mercy.

The Pharisees continue pressing Him for an answer. Finally Jesus raises Himself up and speaks
words that pierce to the center of their granite
hearts, "Let him that is without sin among you cast
the first stone." He then resumes writing on the
ground. Suddenly the clamor stops. There is perfect
silence. No one says a word for there is nothing for
the Pharisees to say. One blow of truth has crushed
the accusations that supported their unforgiveness.

When we're brought before Jesus, the question to

be answered is not who is right and who is wrong. We can be *dead* right! What would the woman have been if the Pharisees had their way? Dead! Jesus is not in the business of killing sinners. The "religious" people do that.

Our mentality about sin and forgiveness causes us to ask the wrong questions. The question is, "Who has the right to throw the first stone?" Jesus was the only one there who had the right and He refused it. None of us are in a position to judge others for their sin, so we're all disqualified from rock throwing. The question we need to ask is, "Who is going to forgive?" It is not a matter of right and wrong; it's a matter of forgiveness!

From the oldest to the youngest they all slither out, dropping their stones behind them. The woman is left alone with Jesus. He straightens Himself up again and says to her, "Woman, where are your accusers?" She stands before the only One who can legitimately condemn her for her sin. Will He? She sees the answer in His wonderful face, for she says, "I don't seem to have any accusers." Jesus says to the woman, "Neither do I condemn you."

If there are no accusers in the church, the only other accuser according to the book of Revelation is the devil. We have a choice: we can side with the accuser of the brethren and throw rocks, or we can agree with the Man Jesus and say, "Neither do I condemn you." Condemnation does not come from God. "For God sent not his Son into the world to condemn the world; but that the world through him might be saved" (John 3:17). In forgiving we reflect the face of Jesus. Our unforgiveness reflects the accuser of the brethren himself.

After telling the woman that He does not condemn her, Jesus says simply, "Go and sin no more." Jesus does more than refuse to condemn the woman. He affirms her in His love. Why didn't Jesus confront the woman with her sin and demand that she repent? The woman had not asked to be forgiven. She just *needed* to be forgiven.

One Greek scholar interprets this passage to more exactly read, "Go and *thou shalt* sin no more." It is more a statement of confidence than a command. Jesus is saying to the woman, "You've been living in sin for years. You have been accused for years; you've been condemned for years. No one believes in you anymore. I forgive you! Receive release from the power of sin to go and sin no more."

I forgive you. Oh, what a power is in those words! Mercy and truth are met together in the face of forgiveness (Psalm 85:10). The power of the law to kill the sinner is swallowed up in the victory of Calvary. As we forgive one another the wonderful compassion of Jesus can be seen in our faces to draw the world to Him.

THE FATHER, THE ELDER BROTHER AND THE PRODIGAL

Look again into the face of forgiveness. It is a tear-stained face, the face of a heart that has grieved over the loss of one who was so dear. It is a yearning face with eyes creased from watching, waiting, longing to see one who is far away. It is a father's face. A father who delights in the children remaining with Him, but who will not be content until the prodigal son returns to his house.

But there is another face in this picture. A frowning face that cannot understand the earnest watching of the father. A resentful face that every day calculates the loss incurred to the household by the inheritance his younger brother so impetuously demanded. How will this elder brother respond if the prodigal son does return? He remembers well his harsh words and the dire predictions he made at their parting.

In the distance a third face can barely be seen, yet it appears to be moving closer to the foreground. What a contrast to the well-groomed father and elder brother. This man is disheveled, his clothes torn and filthy, his face grimy with sweat and dirt. And yet his countenance is somehow familiar. Yes, in some way it resembles the first face, the father's face. The longing in the eyes, the intensity of the gaze. And this face too is stained with tears.

Suddenly a cry pierces the air. "Oh, my son, my son!" A cry of joy, of relief, of compassion as the father runs to meet the one he has been waiting for. The filthy wretch is his own dear son and he flies to embrace him.

But how can he respond this way to one who had treated him with such contempt? The prodigal had just walked away one day. He had rejected his father and mocked the value of being in his father's house. He sought those things that opposed his father's way of life and callously went his way taking half of his father's living. Now that was gone, wasted, never to be recovered.

Our church has experienced this suffering. Some of those who have shared the dream that God had put into our hearts have walked away from us. At times there was financial loss to the church. At first

I complained to the Lord, "Father, Your way is going to allow people to ride rough-shod over us all of our lives." But the Lord said to me, "If you can understand My heart, you can freely forgive anybody of anything." *To see the beauty in the face of forgiveness we must have a revelation of the Father's heart.*

My Father took me to the story of the prodigal. There this man was, snout to snout with a pig, fighting over a corn husk—and he remembered what his father's house was like. The Lord spoke to my heart, "That's all that matters to Me. When they remember what My house was like, I forget all that has happened before. I just want them back in My house and I want you to help me pay the price to get them there." A part of that price is forgiveness.

How many prodigals would be willing to return to the Father's house if they could be sure a warm reception was awaiting them? Sometimes people have gotten themselves into some very difficult situations. What is our response going to be? "Well, if you repent long and loud enough and do everything just right from now on, we might consider letting you back into the Father's house." Fortunately the prodigal son in Jesus' parable was met with quite a different face.

Running to meet his son, the father reaches him while he is still some distance from the house. Though the prodigal is covered with the filth and stench of the pig sty his father falls on his neck and kisses him. With that kiss of greeting the son knows that he is received home again. Before he can speak his well-rehearsed repentance, the father begins showering him with gifts of acceptance: shoes for his naked feet, a robe to cover his filthiness, and the signet ring giving him access once more to his father's treasury. He orders a feast with a fatted calf for the entire household to celebrate the return of his beloved son. They walk arm in arm back into the father's house, the prodigal's face overwhelmed with gratitude, the father's radiant with joy. Everyone is rejoicing.

Everyone except the elder brother. His countenance is as dark as the father's is light. How could the father receive that prodigal back after he had squandered half of their living? And why this ridiculous excess of gifts! While the father is having a party with his younger son, this son is plotting his revenge tactics—pouting, demanding, resenting.

Soon the father misses the elder brother and comes outside to bring him in. This son can hardly bear to look at his father's delighted face. He sullenly remarks, "I've been with you all these years and you never fixed me a calf." The father looks into his son's pained face and tenderly says, "Son, you are always with me, and all that I have is yours."

The Lord gave me revelation of the father's reply that has forever changed my attitude toward returning prodigals. The elder brother never left the father's house. Those of us that have stayed and faithfully served our Father need a revelation of what we have received. A calf, a party, tokens of love and appreciation. Can these be compared to being always with the Father? As I struggled in my heart over my feelings concerning one who had left our church, the Father spoke to me, "All that he has lost in the years he has been away, you have had. All the revelation, all the blessings, all the visitation of My Spirit. He has been in a land of famine.

You have never lacked spiritually for any good thing, and besides all that, you have been with Me—in My presence."

I persisted, "But Lord, what about the money he caused us to lose?" The Lord said to me, "Don't ever mention it. Pay his way back in. You can afford it. Have you ever needed anything that you could not buy? Haven't you and the church prospered financially? Have I not provided well for you?"

If we can understand the magnanimous heart of our Father we will never yield to self-righteousness or resentment. The one who stays with the Father is abundantly wealthy. And the one who returns to the Father is abundantly blessed. Many material things are important to elder brothers. But all that matters to the Father is that when in the pig sty, his erring son remembers what His house is like and wants to return. The Father just wants him back in His house.

> . . . "Joy shall be in heaven over one sinner that repenteth, more than over ninety and nine just persons, which need no repentance" (Luke 15:7).

We can forgive those that have taken from us. We can rejoice over their reunion with the Father and help pay their way back into fellowship with the Father's house by never mentioning the loss. We can behold the beauty of the joy on the Father's face and embrace His way of forgiveness until our countenances beam with the love of His own beautiful face.

Part II

Functioning as the Forgiving Church

6

Full Forgiveness

And be ye kind one to another, tenderhearted, forgiving one another, even as God for Christ's sake hath forgiven you (Ephesians 4:32).

While I was preaching the series of messages on forgiveness that formed the foundation for this book, a member of our congregation came to me and said, "All of the teaching we've received on forgiveness concerns our need to forgive others. Pastor, I wish you would preach sometime to the person whose actions cause me to have to forgive." This need for accountability is the other side of forgiveness.

We invite disaster if we teach a church to walk in forgiveness without requiring responsible living. When we only teach people to forgive, forgive, forgive, we risk placing in their minds the attitude that they can do whatever they wish because others are obligated to forgive them. Everyone—forgivers and forgivees—must live as Christians or we are not properly functioning as the Body of Christ. Careless living makes forgiveness a burden.

A full understanding of forgiveness in the church goes beyond our willingness to forgive one another. We must become aware of the strain our "say whatever we think" and "do whatever we please" approach to life places on our brothers and sisters. If we are going to work together effectively to accomplish the ministry of the church we must become sensitive to those actions and reactions in ourselves that precipitate forgiveness. Then our goal will be to refrain from unduly burdening one another with the need to forgive. The primary precipitator of forgiveness is offense.

OFFENSE

I have become convinced that one half of the Christian world doesn't know how the other half—who are forgiving them—lives. I once heard someone say, "I'm the happiest person in the world!" I thought, "You ought to be. You have everyone around you serving you. You don't have any problems in your life because you've become a problem to everyone else." This person's approach to life engendered offense. Some people will never have strokes or heart attacks themselves—they're just carriers!

Of course some people are offended because we get up in the morning! We are not responsible for people's idiosyncrasies or their unreasonable expectations. I have a friend who pastors a congregation of about fifteen hundred. He's a very sensitive man and truly desires to please God. He told me that members of his church are offended if he cannot personally counsel all of them. Their taking offense is illegitimate because their expectation is unreasonable.

But in our familiarity with one another in the church we sometimes treat each other in ways that are blatantly offensive. Through our insensitivity we become carriers of problems that precipitate forgiveness. People are offended when we take advantage of them: barging ahead of them in line; borrowing their car and using all of the gas; promising that we will be at the prayer meeting to help others intercede and never showing up. We're happy to be caught up on our rest, but they have to pray through *and forgive us* for our irresponsibility. We may pass off such incidences as "little things people understand," but the sting of the offense remains.

Jesus offers His perspective on offenses: "It must needs be that offenses come; but woe to that man by whom the offense cometh!" (Matthew 18:7). The Scripture's command to forgive does not give us a license to offend. If we are going to be balanced in our understanding of forgiveness, we must realize that when we offend, a woe is coming our way. Even when those that we offend forgive us, we can lose their respect. Proverbs 10:26 says that the person who won't do his share of the work is like smoke in his comrades' eyes. "Yes, we'll forgive you for not doing your share, but you make our eyes water . . . in more ways than one."

Habitual offenders have not taken seriously the warning in Proverbs 18:19, "A brother offended is harder to be won than a strong city: and their contentions are like the bars of a castle." If we commit enough unresolved offenses against our brothers and sisters in the church we can finally displace ourselves in the Body of Christ.

A PRE-FORGIVENESS MENTALITY

With its warning against offense, the Bible also offers advice on how we can avoid offending our fellow Christians. Allowing that *offenses will come*, the Scriptures also outline steps for dealing with the offenses that do occur. When we embrace these guidelines for our behavior we are functioning with what I term a "pre-forgiveness mentality."

Live Carefully

In Romans 14 Paul expresses a preventative aspect of the pre-forgiveness mentality. This entire chapter concerns having regard for the weaknesses of other brothers. He advises Christians to be sensitive not to offend them by discounting their beliefs in matters that are not essential to salvation. Included are such admonitions as:

> Accept him whose faith is weak, without passing judgment on disputable matters. Instead, make up your mind not to put any stumbling block or obstacle in your brother's way. Let us therefore make every effort to do what leads to peace and to mutual edification. So whatever you believe about these things keep between yourself and God. (vv. 1, 13b, 19, 22 NIV)

As Christians we are responsible to respect the beliefs and practices of our brothers and sisters. We sin when we flaunt things before people that we know offend their consciences. Anne Gimenez preaches a sermon titled "Don't Tell It All" on being wise in the way we express our beliefs to others. Good advice when you are seeking not to offend!

Those involved in realms of ministry should be particularly aware of the impression their manner makes on others. I once heard Winkie Pratney say that we make our own choices concerning our sphere of influence in ministry. We can choose to be acceptable in the way we dress, act and talk and influence many people; or we can please ourselves in these matters and influence a handful of people. We might argue with his point by thinking that if we are all free in the Lord we ought to be able to do what we want to do. But this attitude really expresses an immaturity in choosing to please ourselves over desiring to reach others. Being careful in the way we live our lives before others demonstrates our cooperation with the scriptural injunction to esteem our brothers more highly than we do ourselves (Philippians 2:3).

Take Responsibility

But what if we do offend someone? Jesus details how we should respond.

> Therefore if thou bring thy gift to the altar, and there rememberest that thy brother hath ought against thee; Leave there thy gift before the altar, and go thy way; first be reconciled to thy brother, and then come and offer thy gift (Matthew 5:23-24).

We have not begun to grow in forgiveness until we become responsible to the people we have offended. We may say, "Well, that's their problem if they are offended." No, it's the church's problem. And it's our problem. God doesn't hear the prayer of the person who is not walking in the light with his brother. Many churches don't realize that this is what is wrong with their prayer lives. They keep offering the gift, offering the gift, offering the gift. But God is not accepting it. Their broken relationships with their brothers have created a barrier of unforgiveness more destructive to the church than the wiles of the devil. God requires that our relationships be right with one another before we can commune freely with Him.

"First be reconciled." This doesn't mean to go and say empty words, merely admitting that there is a problem. "Well, I guess you know that things haven't been right between us. We need to just do the best we can. You know how hard you are to get along with." We have not repented unless *we have taken the responsibility* to be truly reconciled to one another.

Our excuses for not obeying this admonition are countless. Some people are afraid they will offend someone in asking his forgiveness. How much can we offend a person by asking him to forgive us for an offense? We must take the risk! "But I'm afraid he might misunderstand." How could he misunderstand our simply saying, "I offended you. Please forgive me." If someone is offended by that, he is not responding as a brother in Christ. We are freed from the fear of going to one another by desiring the fruit of reconciliation above all else in our lives.

We can reap another blessed fruit by going to our brother to be reconciled. Did you ever pray, "Humble me, God. Oh, humble me!" Don't waste time praying that way—the scripture says for us to humble ourselves (James 4:10). Asking people to forgive us is one of the greatest ways to humble ourselves for it is absolutely against our prideful makeup. As we humble ourselves to be reconciled to our brothers, we are fulfilling the first step of taking responsibility in our relationships.

Agree Quickly

Jesus strengthens His command for reconciliation by adding:

> Agree with thine adversary quickly, whiles thou art in the way with him; lest at any time the adversary deliver thee to the judge, and the judge deliver thee to the officer, and thou be cast into prison. Verily I say to thee, Thou shalt by no means come out thence, till thou has paid the uttermost farthing (Matthew 5:25-26).

Jesus emphasized that we are to agree quickly. What is our response? We want to pray about it first. Iverna Tompkins says, "God can speak something to a person face to face, and what does he respond? I want a confirmation." Don't pray about it—agree quickly as Jesus has commanded.

Agree quickly. Why? The scripture tells us that if we do not act quickly we will be required to pay the last penny. I've paid a few "last pennies." Do you know why I didn't agree quickly? Because I was right! Holding on to being right is one of the most foolish things we can do. The Lord said to me, "Go ahead, be right—and see where being right gets you!" It dawned on me that I could be right and still end up being the loser.

Once a man in our congregation felt that I needed to ask his forgiveness. There were several things relating to his life that he thought I should have handled differently. I could see his point to a certain extent, but I didn't fully agree with him. So even though we had a somewhat amicable relationship there was an intellectual battle going on: he was requiring that I ask his forgiveness for these things and I was resisting agreeing with him.

The Lord spoke to me, "Agree with everything he has against you and you will be free." I still thought the man was requiring too much of me, but the Lord said, "What do you have to lose? It's in the past and you can't go back and do things differently. Agree with him." It didn't matter who was right or wrong. What really mattered was getting rid of the bondage our unresolved relationship was causing the church.

So I met with the man and said, "You know, things just don't seem to be right between us. Something is out of order." He then began to list his grievances against me. For each thing he brought up I said, "You're right, I wish I had handled that another way. I want to ask your forgiveness for being insensitive in that situation." Even though I didn't feel responsible for all of his complaints, I gave room that I could have been completely at fault. When I did that, a real freedom was brought to the situation and our relationship was restored.

At first I felt too righteous to allow myself to be completely at fault. But after God broke through on my heart, being right didn't matter anymore. Now when I look back on it, I can definitely see his side of the matter. The more I have thought about it, the more right I think he was!

In our pride we do not want to agree fully, to say we were totally at fault. This agitates our "adversary"—the one we have offended—and leaves room for the devil to plant a distrust of us in his mind.

Admitting our fault will not discredit us to the person as we fear it will. If we humble ourselves and take the blame, we can restore his trust in us.

Because I didn't agree quickly I had to pay the last penny. If I had agreed with the man in the beginning, I would not have had to go through the session where he pointed out every little thing he felt that I had done to offend him. The final outcome was a much more costly agreement than the initial situation would have required.

If we agree quickly, offenses can be resolved in general terms. But if we insist on being right, we may find our feet held to the fire. Instead of trying to wriggle our way out of accepting blame, we can choose to agree. Both we and our adversary will go free at much less cost to us!

Examine Ourselves

In the Lord's Prayer, the section on forgiving those who offend us is followed by a prevenient prayer: Lead us not into temptation, but deliver us from evil. A pre-forgiveness mentality involves preventative living—diffusing potential difficulties before the need for forgiveness arises. As a part of that prevention we should examine our own lives to discover if we are recognizing unforgiveness in ourselves.

Many of our ordinary expressions are actually euphemisms for unforgiveness: We don't put so-and-so with so-and-so; they "don't get along." We refer to "personality clashes" as a normal expectation in certain relationships. These attitudes mark our acceptance of unforgiveness because we don't love each other enough to confront our difficulties. When enough of these unforgiving attitudes are working, the sweetness goes right out of a congregation. We excuse unforgiveness by merely tolerating one another and in the process become hypocrites.

We don't usually identify bad moods as unforgiveness, but sarcasm, cutting comments, negative speaking and even grouchiness can be signs of an unforgiving nature. Did you ever wake up in the morning feeling like a thundercloud had settled over your bed? You woke up with an unforgiving attitude.

Our gloomy moods can also be states of unforgiveness. We don't forgive God for making us the way He did. We don't forgive those around us for making our lives the way they are. We don't forgive people in our past for giving us the memories we have. Most of us don't realize how much unforgiveness we walk around with on a continual basis. Yet we Christians say we are a forgiving people. We mean if things get bad enough and we are confronted, we will finally cough up a forgiveness!

Sometimes our unforgiveness is buried deep within. We can even say that we forgive people and act kind and loving but deep in our hearts not release them from the negative feelings, thoughts and attitudes we have toward them. We can sometimes become so accustomed to tolerating unforgiving attitudes in ourselves that we are totally blind to our own hypocrisy.

The only safeguard against deception in the realm of forgiveness is to open our hearts for examination. I evaluate myself by asking if I feel toward a person the way I did the last time the Holy Spirit brought deep repentance in my heart. The Holy Spirit is the only one who can tell us the real truth about our need to forgive. Bob Mumford says, "We keep trying to crucify ourselves, but we use rubber nails. Let

Jesus do it. He's a carpenter." We need to pray as David did, "Examine me and see if there is any wicked way in me." Our hearts require daily cleansing if we are to maintain an attitude of forgiveness in the living of our lives.

A further aid to recognizing unforgiveness in ourselves is to ask another person to evaluate our feelings and responses in a matter. If we assume that our thoughts and attitudes are usually correct, we are setting ourselves up for hidden unforgiveness. Through this self-righteous attitude we may experience the embarrassment of being people whom others recognize as unforgiving but will not tell us for fear of our rebuff.

Leaders especially need to keep themselves open to input from their peers. We can become very harsh and boastful, confident and self-assured that we know all of the answers. Perhaps those who teach and lead are in greater danger of harboring hidden unforgiveness, settling into the notion that we are the tellers and others are the listeners. In matters concerning forgiveness, all must be willing to listen.

If we function with a pre-forgiveness mentality we are sensitive to the causes and effects of unforgiveness. We determine that no relationship in the body of Christ will deteriorate. That doesn't mean that everyone in the church will be our best friend. Obviously we will be closer to some than others. Some people will do things that we don't like and we must face the fact that forgiving them will not automatically change their personalities! But we can develop a habit of continually thinking forgiveness in life's minor irritations: forgiving people for wearing clothes we don't care for, talking in manners which irritate us, and having tastes or habits opposed to our own.

Full forgiveness embraces both sides of the offense issue. We must continually submit our hearts to God and our responses to others to make sure we are not tolerating attitudes of unforgiveness in ourselves. And by taking responsibility in our relationships to agree quickly with our adversary, we can close the door on offense and its more deadly offspring—bitterness.

BITTERNESS

When offenses are not dealt with and resolved, a person's heart becomes open to bitterness. Hebrews 12:15 says, "See to it that no one misses the grace of God and that no bitter root grows up to cause trouble, thereby defiling many" (NIV). *Offenses plant the seed that grows the root of bitterness.*

Jesus teaches that when we come to pray and realize that we have offended someone, we are to be reconciled with that person before we offer our prayer. So if we were scriptural, how often would we make sure that any offense was made right? At least as often as we prayed or came to a worship service. The problem with prolonged offenses is that they turn into bitterness. The scripture is admonishing us to halt the process in the offense stage, to dig up the seed of offense before the bitter root can grow.

In dealing with bitter roots, I have observed that *offense* is the element that turns the heart. It usually isn't a single offense that turns someone's heart but rather the *last* offense. For example, a family just loves the church, the pastor, the vision of the work—everything is right. Then one day they seem to flip over to side two. Nothing is done to suit them, they take exception to the preaching, they wonder where the church is going—everything is wrong. On side two everything is perceived through the filter of offense. Even overtures for reconciliation are colored by their bitterness. People in this condition often leave the church and their memories of negative experiences can keep them from becoming a part of another fellowship of believers. Only deep repentance, a work of the Holy Spirit, can pull up the bitter root the seed of offense has grown.

Besides individual casualties, a bitter root presents a significant threat to the church. We have the promise of God's Word that if a bitter root is allowed to grow up, *it will defile many*. Why? Because the bitter person will share his bitterness. Even if he doesn't discuss the specific offense that caused him to become bitter, his negative attitude will have a defiling influence on other members of the congregation because he is a bitter person.

Given the difficulty in displacing bitter roots and their danger to the church, we can appreciate the urgency of the admonition, "See to it that . . . no bitter root grows up." When I minister this scripture to pastors, I remind them that since they have the care of the flock, they have the first responsibility to "see to it." But the book of Hebrews was not written to pastors only. All Christians have the responsibility to see that no one fails of the grace of God and that no bitter root grows up and defiles another. Any church member who is aware of the possibility of a bitter root springing up should "see to it." We are all accountable and charged by the Word of the Lord: See to it! This is the forgiving church, one that does not allow bitter roots to develop.

Anger

What does the scripture actually mean when it tells us to "see to it"? Our normal response is that we cannot keep people from being bitter if they choose to be. But the scripture is assuming that we can. We may not be able to prevent the offense that allows the possibility of a bitter root, but we can take steps to keep it from taking hold in a person's heart. This effort begins with our recognition that bitterness has its basis in anger.

The Hebrew word translated "bitter" in the Old Testament is *marah*. The essential meaning of this word is *a trickling or distillation of anger or discontentment*. It conveys an idea similar to the Chinese water torture: drip . . . drip . . . drip. Distillation refines an element into its purest form. Bitterness is distilled anger: anger brought to the point of deep, resolved hatred and enmity.

The Greek word translated "bitter" in the New Testament is *pikraino* defined as *a piercingly angry attitude or a resolve to be angry; a resolved anger*. It carries the understanding of driving in tent stakes and setting up camp over the anger. This sense of permanence is in contrast to the nature of anger as defined by Webster: a strong but *usually temporary* feeling of displeasure. Anger in itself is not so terrible. The scripture tells us to be angry and sin not. But it also warns not to let the sun go down on our wrath. Unresolved anger moves to bitterness; then we as the church have a problem.

We find an avenue for avoiding bitter roots by helping people properly deal with their anger. Psychologists tell us that anger stems from hurt, fear, or frustration. Looking at the underlying causes of anger helps us identify and deal with a person's real need.

A person may respond to something that hurts him by becoming angry. In offering a truthful explanation of the situation in the light of God's grace to forgive we can help someone to resolve his anger. We can teach him to release forgiveness to cleanse the anger and prevent it from distilling into bitterness.

A person may appear to be angry who is really afraid. We should pray for sensitivity to discern a person's fear that may be underlying his angry words. In helping him to identify his fear we can diffuse the anger and aid a person in voicing his real needs.

Frustration stems from disappointed goals and blocked desires. Someone may become angry and finally bitter toward the leadership of the church if his expectations are disappointed or his plans for his life are frustrated. His frustration may really be with God. In that case he needs to be taught both God's care and His sovereignty. Developing a trust in God precludes the debilitating forces of fear and frustration.

The serious consequences of anger turned to bitterness are demonstrated in the sad saga of Esau. When Esau found that he had lost his father's blessing, he cried out with a bitter cry (Genesis 27:34). He resolved to kill his brother Jacob for displacing him (v. 41). Esau was frustrated, his expectation was disappointed. He was angry and that anger became a grudge, a bitterness against his brother.

The New Testament commentary on Esau says that he could not find a place of repentance, even though he sought it with tears (Hebrews 12:17). Could it be that Esau's unforgiveness toward his brother contributed to the hardness of heart that kept him from repentance? We cannot be truly repentant before God as long as we have judgments and bitter unforgiveness against our brothers. Unresolved anger can eventually remove a person from the Kingdom of God. We cannot serve God with the bondage of bitterness in our lives.

Bitter Root Judgments

Bitter root judgments categorize people according to a person's negative experience. I once worked with a woman that said, "Men are not fit to live." At that time I had not been married very long, but the man that I lived with seemed to me very fit to live! I couldn't understand why a woman would say such a thing. Obviously her experiences with a man or some men had embittered her and she had formed a bitter root judgment against all men. Though it was not true, it clouded everything that was in her life. What was the basic problem? Unforgiveness. She did not forgive the offense. It grew into bitterness and it would have defiled me if I had allowed it.

We unwittingly make all kinds of bitter root judgments: "That's how people are!" "He says he'll do that, but can you trust him?" Our responses are based on the fact that somebody else let us down. Through the prejudice of bitter root judgments we cripple our relationships in the body of Christ. We need to see one another as God sees us—as individuals with distinct histories and destinies. In so doing our loads of bitterness would greatly diminish and the "gift of suspicion" would cease to function in the church.

Guarding Our Hearts

The Moravians had a rather unusual rule in their church, but it proved most effective for them. If anyone brought before the elders a list of grievances that they had held towards someone over a long period of time, *the person who brought the grievances* was dismissed from the church. It would seem that the one who had offended should be disciplined, but the Moravians believed that one who had held unforgiveness, and thus lived in sin for so long, had demonstrated his unwillingness to be a part of the body of Christ. We must take the responsibility to guard our own hearts from bitter roots.

I often would fellowship with a certain couple in our church after the Sunday evening service. After a time my schedule changed and I had not been with them for several weeks. The man came to me and said, "Sue, I noticed that you haven't invited yourself over in quite a while. Is there anything wrong, have we offended you?" I explained about the change in my schedule and he understood. I really appreciated the sensitivity he had to see that no bitter root would grow up. He approached me gently, with a positive attitude and the matter was settled.

In "seeing to it" that no bitter root grows we must see to our own hearts. We must diligently be on guard against the offense, anger and suspicion that grow the root of bitterness. If we sense that someone is acting differently toward us, instead of getting bitter, we should get an answer.

Bitterness is one of the devil's greatest weapons against the Body of Christ, but forgiveness protects our own hearts and those of our brothers and sisters from such attacks. We are our brother's keeper. The New Testament adjures us to look not only after our own interests, but to look "also to the interests of others" (Philippians 2:4 NIV). In the case of bitterness, an individual can be lost to the cause of Christ if his brothers and sisters do not rescue him from its entanglements. It is the responsibility of the church and especially of the leadership to see to it that bitter roots do not have an opportunity to grow. Forgiveness is the tool that the Lord has given us to uproot the deadly plant that sprouts from the seeds of offense.

7

False Forgiveness

> They have healed also the hurt of the daughter of
> my people slightly, saying, Peace, peace; when there
> is no peace (Jeremiah 6:14).

The messages of the New Testament speak of
"missing the mark" or falling short of the provisions
God has made for us to walk together in His kingdom. The primary hindrance to our functioning as
the Forgiving Church is not blatant unforgiveness.
It is not that we adamantly refuse to forgive. We
fall short of God's provision by settling for false forgiveness.

The truth of forgiveness is central to the Gospel of
Jesus Christ. Therefore, it would seem impossible for
a Christian not to have this reality functioning in
his life. But like the word *love, forgive* has become a
blanket term used to identify a broad spectrum of
emotions and responses. We can toss out "I forgive
you" as thoughtlessly as we do "Have a nice day."
This shallow application leaves us with something
worse than unforgiveness: we are deceived into thinking that we have forgiven when we have not.

False forgiveness counterfeits a work of the Spirit. Words are spoken and certain advances and approaches are made but the breach made by offense and unforgiveness is not mended. It is a "that's alright, I forgive you, we won't talk about it anymore" shallow facade of forgiveness that passes things off with a word but does not effect a healing in the wounded hearts of those involved. While the matter may appear to be settled, God is looking upon the hearts of His children filled with burdens that our surface approach of false forgiveness can never release. The remedy for unforgiveness is profoundly simple: repent and forgive. The subtle forms of false forgiveness require that we carefully examine the motivation and fruit of an act of forgiveness to be sure it is genuine.

Forgiveness is not for the purpose of letting us off the hook or easing our consciences. It is a gift that God purchased for us on the cross of Calvary. It is the liberating power of Jesus' blood that sets men free from the inside out! Jesus died for the reality of our being delivered from bitterness, jealousy, and offenses. The provision of forgiveness allows us to reopen the lines of communication until our hearts are truly in touch with each other again. Forgiveness is the entrance to a work of God that is ultimately consummated in restoration.

WHOLE FORGIVENESS

The goal of forgiveness is restoration—restoration of relationships, restoration of fellowship with God and within the church. Our heavenly Father completes the work He begins. He doesn't leave His children wounded and crippled. Jesus said to the man at the pool of Bethesda, "Wilt thou be made whole?" (John 5:6). He did not use the Greek word *therapeuo*, the essence of which means "not sick." The word translated whole in this scripture is *hugiaino* which means "to wax or to come to a place of strength." In the vernacular Jesus might have asked, "Do you want to be put together?" or "Do you want to be through with what is wrong with you?" The scripture then records that Jesus said, "Rise, take up your bed, and walk!"

God does not heal people so they can stay in bed. Likewise, He has not ministered forgiveness so that we remain crippled in our souls and spirits. God has given us a plan for wholeness in our relationships that begins when we walk through the doorway of forgiveness. But we don't stop walking until the work of reconciliation is accomplished so that on the other side we can be made whole—completely restored.

Step One—Forgiveness

Forgiveness opens the door. We make the decision to loose our brother from our negative opinions and attitudes. This transaction occurs within our own hearts in the presence of God. Before we ever approach the person we are forgiving, we must seal the choice to forgive in our own will.

We do not forgive in order to "get something off of our chest." In forgiving we offer the release that stands back from the situation and says, "I am not willing to hold my brother in bondage." We determine not to be negative toward him anymore and we release him to be blessed by God and by us.

Forgiveness is the step that looses us from unforgiveness that we might be reconciled with our brother.

Step Two—Reconciliation

Through reconciliation the process of forgiveness is manifested in the church. We go to the other person, discuss the difficulty and find a place of agreement in God. But reconciliation goes beyond words, beyond saying, "I forgive you, I loose you." We then begin to develop a sincere relationship with the person so that we can work with him, pray with him and help to build his life, his home and his ministry in the church. Reconciliation is seeing things as one. When we are again walking together "in the light" then we can achieve the final step of restoration.

Step Three—Restoration

Forgiveness is the *door* and reconciliation is the *means* to accomplish the *goal* of restoration. Through forgiveness we deal with the past, releasing the person from what he did. Reconciliation deals with the present relationship, permitting harmony in the living of our lives together. But restoration goes a step further. It secures a future for our relationships in the church. To restore means "to bring back to the former condition." Through restoration we recover that essential element which was lost through the wounds of offense and unforgiveness—*trust.*

At times we may have made a concerted effort to repair a broken relationship. We said that we had forgiven someone, but we knew in our hearts that things would never really be the same between us, that we would never really trust the person again. Yet we still insist that we have forgiven him. If we are not going to trust him again, why pretend that we have forgiven? If we can't give him another chance, what is redemption about? Our God is the God of new beginnings! He allows us to start all over again. There may be consequences to our mistakes, but He will help us through those too. He wants us to have a fresh start. The goal of the process of forgiveness is for all to be able to say, "Come back into my heart as if it had never happened."

Many times I have sinned against the Father and I've lain on the floor and wept, crying, "Take me back, Father, take me back." I don't want Him to receive me at arm's length; I don't want Him to put me on probation. I want to crawl into my Father's arms again, to feel His love. I want to know that the sin that was separating us has been put under the blood of Jesus and I can be in rich communion and fellowship with Him as I was before. "Take me back, take me back." I believe that true forgiveness is taking each other back into our hearts.

Though forgiveness restores heart affection, in all cases relationships will not be restored *positionally*. A man and woman who have divorced do not have to remarry to experience heartfelt forgiveness for one another. In some cases this would be undesirable or impossible. If a church leader has been released from his office because of severe sin in his life the congregation can genuinely forgive him, but he would not resume his position solely on the basis of their forgiveness. The further work of restoration he needs ministered to him is of a different nature than the restoration of heart affection. There are even times when a relationship needs to be adjusted for true restoration to take place. Forgiveness supercedes temporal circumstances. It's a matter of the heart.

HALFWAY FORGIVENESS

To begin the process of forgiveness and stop short of full restoration leaves the person needing forgiveness in limbo. He's in the church, participating in the activities, fulfilling the expectations. But because his relationships in the church have not been secured through heart forgiveness he feels that his future is always in question. This halfway forgiveness can be worse than none at all. In the life of David we can see the tragic consequences of a halfway forgiveness.

David's son Absalom killed his own brother Amnon because Amnon had raped their sister Tamar. Then Absalom fled to a neighboring country where he remained, banished from his father's house. After three years Joab, David's general, sought to reconcile David with his son. He arranged for the woman of Takoah to come and tell a story to David. She told how one of her two sons had killed his brother and that the people were coming to kill the son that was left. The woman cried for mercy and said, "My husband is dead, I have no other sons. There will be no one to carry on the lineage of the family. Don't let this thing happen." David said, "Of course your son should not be killed. You should not be left without a son." Then she said to David, "My lord, I am speaking of your son." And Joab begged David to allow Absalom to return.

David said to Joab, "Very well, I will do it. Go, bring back the young man Absalom. [But] he must go to his own house; *he must not see my face*" (2 Samuel 14:21, 23 NIV). David was not opposed to Absalom's return from exile, but he refused to restore his relationship with him as the king's son. "Absalom lived two years in Jerusalem without seeing the king's face" (v. 28 NIV).

After this period of time Absalom began to seethe under this halfway forgiveness. He did a few things to get Joab's attention, like setting his ripe barley field on fire. Has anyone ever set your field on fire? People in the church who are laboring under the burden of a halfway forgiveness will do all manner of strange things. They are conveying a message born of desperation: "Is anybody going to really forgive me?" I believe that God allows these things to come against the church when we fail to complete the process of forgiveness.

The field-burning incident succeeded in getting Joab's attention. Absalom clearly states his complaint to Joab.

> Look, I sent word to you and said, "Come here so I can send you to the king to ask, 'Why have I come from Geshur? It would be better for me if I were still there!' " Now then, I want to see the king's face, and if I am guilty of anything, let him put me to death (v. 32 NIV).

Please understand that I am no fan of Absalom. I have no respect for a person who would undermine his father's authority as he later did. But recognize with me this picture of a halfway forgiveness. He simply said, "I want to see the king's face, and if he still thinks I'm guilty, then let him kill me." It appears that Absalom was willing to die rather than to endure a halfway forgiveness. We don't realize the torment we place people in when we say in effect, "Come on back to Jerusalem, but you can't see my face." "Come on back to church. I'll tolerate you, but I won't love you." A halfway forgiveness can be worse than death.

Some Christians have misunderstood restoration

and believe they are condoning a person's sin if they receive them back into fellowship in the church without qualifications. They fear that by warmly receiving their fellow Christian who has failed, they will make him think that he has done nothing wrong and their accepting him will give him license to continue in his wrong doing. In restoring people we are not condoning their sin. We are celebrating the new beginning that forgiveness offers everyone.

Other Christians think that God needs help with vengeance so they help God judge a person by withholding their approval and affection. This posture stems from the conclusion, "If I forgive that fellow, the next thing you know God may give him some kind of gift. If he begins to think that he's okay, he'll start getting really free and before you know it, he'll come out of this before he's paid for it."

We wouldn't mind restoring people and asking God to bless them if we were sure that He was going to judge them *first*. God is not like we are. He gives whole forgiveness. If we are waiting around for God to take revenge for our sake, we had better make sure that we have plenty of food with us or we'll starve to death!

Our reluctance to restore people sometimes stems from our thinking that because they have sinned we are better than they are. This mentality perpetuates our "one-up" version of false forgiveness. "Being the magnanimous person that I am, I think that I can forgive you. After all, I am spiritually mature and I am used to swallowing a whole lot of things. I can shoulder this heavy burden—along with so many other things I have shouldered for you. Therefore I am willing to forgive you one more time." It's a false forgiveness. We're not reconciled; we're better.

We trust ourselves so much more than we trust other people. This trusting of ourselves is not warranted. We need salvation as much as those we must forgive. If a person's sin is under Jesus' blood, is he not as justified before God as the person that did not sin? Doctrinally we know that this is true, but we do not forgive as though it were. When Christians act on this reality we can have complete restoration in the church.

In the end David's heart was touched by his son's plea to see him.

> The king summoned Absalom, and he came in and bowed down with his face to the ground before the king. And the king kissed Absalom (v. 33 NIV).

With the kiss Absalom finally saw his father's face. The consummation of the work of forgiveness is marked by a kiss. Forgiveness cannot be only an act of obedience—it must be a kiss, an embracing of the heart that restores trust and affection. Without this "kiss" a person is going to yearn to see our face. His yearning will either become a constant pining or he will start setting fields on fire. People cannot be expected to tolerate a halfway forgiveness from brothers and sisters in the church.

Following the kiss, David did trust Absalom again. Unfortunately Absalom chose to betray his father; the story ends with the death of the son and the heartbreak of the father. Our carnal minds respond, "Yeah, that's what I'm afraid will happen to me if I let people back into my heart. They'll just break it again." As forgiving Christians we must be willing for that to happen. The Lord dwells with those who have contrite hearts (Psalm 34:18). It is the heart of one that is willing to humble himself without a guarantee that things will go his way. This is the heart of our forgiving Father.

In the story of the prodigal, another estranged son was kissed by his father. The father received the prodigal back again without reservation, no questions asked. He ran to meet his son with the very best that he had: the robe, the ring, the shoes. But first of all he gave him the kiss—the restoration of heart affection.

HEART FORGIVENESS

Jesus makes clear the nature of the forgiveness He demands from those who call themselves His servants: "This is how my heavenly Father will treat each of you unless you forgive your brothers from your heart" (Matthew 18:35 NIV). We can determine the depth of our forgiveness by our heart affection. In our heart affection, do we really love the people we say we have forgiven?

If we withhold heart forgiveness we actually cooperate with the plans of the enemy. The world has a saying, "With friends like these, who needs enemies?" In the church, with unforgiving saints, who needs a devil? If we lack the power to restore our own members, we will remain lame in our efforts to take the gospel of the kingdom to a world desperate for the message of forgiveness. Without this forgiveness from the heart we will never become the forgiving church.

We must find the way to forgive from our hearts. Keith Green sang a song that says, "What can be done for an old heart like mine? Soften it Lord, with Your oil and Your wine." Only God can turn hard hearts of stone into soft hearts of flesh. The need to

have our hearts softened by God does not diminish—
it increases! As we mature as individual Christians
and as churches we will find our capacity to forgive
stretched to its limits. And eventually we will face a
demand to forgive that exceeds our ability. As the
demand to forgive increases, so must our drawing
on the supernatural grace of God. We as a church
have experienced these stretchings. Through them I
have identified three keys to enlarging our capacity
to forgive from the heart. Each one answers a particular place of testing regarding forgiveness.

Faith

Our ability to forgive is tested by the sheer number and repetition of offenses. Frustration and dis-
couragement can leave us with a "what's the use?"
attitude. Jesus taught his disciples to forgive their
brothers as many times as they trespassed against
them (Luke 17:3-4). To this command they replied,
"Increase our faith!" (v. 5). If we are going to forgive
from the heart, we must have an increase of faith.
We must believe that when we forgive a person, God
enters the situation with the purpose of changing it.
Too often our hearts are discouraged by unbelief:
"Forgiving him doesn't make any difference. He's
never going to change." We need a work of faith in
our hearts to believe that forgiveness does work—that
it will effect what God intends it to. Every other
aspect of our walk before God as Christians demands
faith. Why shouldn't forgiveness? It's the most God-
like thing we can do.

The Cross

Our capacity to forgive is also tested by negative
circumstances that we are helpless to alter. How do

we remain soft and forgiving in the midst of the
bitter experiences that come to us as Christians—
when we've been lied about, taken advantage of,
betrayed? I have been tempted and have almost
chosen to become bitter. But I knew that because I
was called to serve Jesus, bitterness was a luxury I
could not afford. The Lord showed me His answer
for our bitter experiences.

When Moses and the children of Israel came to
the bitter waters (Exodus 15) God provided a means
for making the bitter waters sweet. He showed
Moses a certain tree to cast into the bitter waters;
immediately the water was fit to drink. There is not
enough sweetness in our intellects or carnal natures
to heal our "bitter waters." But God has provided a
Tree that can sweeten our bitter experiences—the
cross of Calvary.

We can put the cross of Jesus into our bitter experience and He can make every bitter thing sweet. The
presence of the cross changes our perspective, for by
embracing the cross we enter into the fellowship of
His sufferings. The reward of that fellowship dis-
solves our resistance to the negative circumstance.
Even though we continue to be buffeted from without, we are no longer victims but victors as we
realize the eternal triumph of life over death. We
can't change the circumstances of our bitter situations, but we can change what they *mean.* And we
can use the sweetness that Jesus brings as a platform from which to preach the wonders of forgiveness that have been worked in our lives.

The Spirit of Love

What can we do when our love runs out? What if
we must honestly identify our heart emotion toward

a person as hate? I once found myself wrestling with this dilemma. A person had hurt me and brought some painful circumstances into my life. I had to confess that for the first time in my life I hated someone. I was ashamed. I did everything I knew to do to bring forth love and forgiveness in my heart for this person, but still there was none.

The Lord showed me the scriptures in 1 John that plainly say you cannot love God and hate your brother; further, if you hate your brother, you are a murderer and no murderer has eternal life. I became desperate in realizing the seriousness of my heart situation. I had identified this as hatred. I couldn't have it!

While in the midst of this inner turmoil, I was in New Zealand ministering to 150 Christian women leaders and pastors' wives. I was teaching them the principles of revival when the Holy Spirit walked into the convention hall that night and put us all on our faces. The women went to one another weeping and then stood to publicly confess their sins. They experienced gut-level repentance. It was Holy Ghost revival!

And there I was with what I had identified as hatred in my heart. With my face pressed into the carpet I cried to the Lord, "God, I'm supposed to be leading these people and I have this hatred in my heart that I can't get rid of. Oh, God, I've come to the end of my love. No matter how hard I try, I can't forgive. I just can't." Then the Lord spoke to me, "What you need is a fresh infilling of the Holy Ghost." He flashed across my mind the verse in Romans 5, "The love of God is shed abroad in our hearts by the Holy Ghost which is given to us." The Holy Ghost *which is given!*

I said, "Oh, hallelujah! *You can give me* the Holy Ghost who will cause the love to be in my heart." I stayed on my face before the Lord until He shed His love abroad in my heart once more. Love that I did not have was created for the one for whom I had felt such hatred. When our love runs out there is a Holy Ghost, and He is given to those who ask.

We are not abandoned to our unforgiving attitudes. God has provided three supernatural ways to prepare our hearts to forgive: faith for our unbelief, the tree of Calvary for our bitter waters, and the Spirit of love shed abroad in our hearts by the Holy Ghost for our hatred. We must reach out and touch God afresh, rather than continually trying to tap our human resources. When we receive a fresh infilling of the Holy Spirit, heart forgiveness comes in the package!

8

Formula for Forgiveness

Let us therefore follow after the things which make for peace, and things wherewith one may edify another (Romans 14:19).

If we have been convinced of the responsibility Christians have to forgive from their hearts we must discover the actions that will make our attitude of forgiveness tangible. Christianity is not a philosophy; it's a life. And our lifestyles must reflect our beliefs or we are the "sounding brass and tinkling cymbals" depicted in 1 Corinthians 13.

GAINING OUR BROTHER

In Matthew 18:15-17 Jesus outlines a three step process for restoring a brother who is in need of our forgiveness. He terms this effort "gaining your brother." But before we examine the plan Jesus gave we need to examine our hearts. Do we care enough to gain our brother? Do we consider it worth the effort? We are willing to travel the world to make one "raw" convert. It thrills us when someone is saved and forgiven of his sins. Yet sometimes we are not willing to go across the street to restore our brother who knows Jesus but presently needs our forgiveness. If our churches are going to be united with the power of agreement necessary to win the lost we must first be willing to gain our brother.

Step One—Confrontation

Moreover if thy brother shall trespass against thee, go and tell him his fault between thee and him alone: if he shall hear thee, thou hast gained thy brother (Matthew 18:15).

The first step in gaining our brother is to speak to him about the difficulty *alone*. But which do we best relate to—Jesus' teaching or the following scenario?

"Hey, Maggie. Where's my chain saw?"

"Ralph borrowed it."

"This is the fourth time this has happened. That guy never brings back anything he borrows. I tell you, Ralph really needs prayer."

The scripture doesn't tell us to go to our pastor, our spouse, our best friend, or our counsellor. It tells us to go to the one who committed the trespass. When it comes to confrontation most of us prefer to stay in the middle of the road. Have you ever thought about what is most often found in the middle of the road? Yellow lines and dead chickens. Cowardice is no excuse for not obeying the word and way of God.

"But he never would receive me!" We tell ourselves that confrontation would only make matters worse. Our aversion to confrontation may be that *we have confused confrontation with accusation.* We are not instructed to accuse our brothers; that's the devil's job. We aren't called to deliver bad news to make them defensive. We are to minister to their need for truth from a platform of love. "But speaking the truth in love [we] may grow up into him in all things, which is the head, even Christ" (Ephesians 4:15).

Confrontation is not a contest of wills where we force our brother to admit that he is wrong so we can be declared right. Our goal is not to make him "shape up," it is to *gain our brother.* The NIV translation reads, "If he listens to you, you have won your brother over." We are going to him for the purpose of restoring fellowship within the church. If he is restored, we've won.

We must determine to grow up, to humble our prideful natures. We must come to the place where we have enough Christian courage to talk to one another as if we really were brothers and not enemies! All of us will have our share of situations that require confrontation.

Step Two—Persuasion

But what if he doesn't receive you? Jesus gives the next step we are to take.

> But if he will not hear thee, then take with thee one or two more, that in the mouth of two or three witnesses every word may be established (Matthew 18:16).

We are prideful to think that if someone won't listen to us they won't listen to anyone. It may be that our temperament isn't compatible with his. Give the guy a break! See if he will listen to someone else. Give him every opportunity, but don't give up on him. Now don't take one or two hot-heads and don't take your best friend. Take people that he will respect, people of humility and prayer. The goal is still to gain your brother.

Step Three—Discipline

And what if he won't listen to the ones we bring with us? We still cannot dismiss the issue.

And if he shall neglect to hear them, tell it to the church. (Matthew 18:17).

This means to bring the issue to trial. If a brother refuses to be reconciled to individual members of the congregation, then the matter must be brought to the leadership of the church.

This requirement is not legalistic. It is God's long-suffering and mercy. Sometimes people will receive correction from the pastor and elders when they won't from fellow sheep. Again the goal is to restore them into fellowship in the church where we can minister to their needs.

In the process of confrontation and persuasion we will find two types of people: those that will hear and those that won't. I call the first category fault-tellable. These people will receive us; they want to be reconciled; we gain our brothers. There are people in our church that I feel free to speak to concerning anything about themselves. I have this liberty because they want to hear from God and they appreciate the care of their pastor.

Then there is the second category of people: they are not interested in hearing from anybody. They don't feel responsible to the Body of Christ. They won't listen to us, the ones we've taken with us, or the leadership of the church. Jesus' answer to these cases was:

> But if he neglect to hear the church, let him be unto thee as a heathen man and a publican (v. 17).

If a person absolutely refuses the ministry of the church, there is no more that we can do. We must not beat ourselves to death. The scripture admonishes us, "If it be possible, as much as lieth in you, live peaceably with all men" (Romans 12:18). When we have tried to bring reconciliation and it is refused, the scripture tells us that the offending party must be counted as an unbeliever. A person who is so obstinate that he will not listen to his brother, other Christians or the leaders of the church can no longer be treated as a believer. He has removed himself from fellowship with the church.

Christians do not have the prerogative to walk in unforgiveness. If we would follow Jesus' admonition in this matter many church splits could be avoided. Most divisions within churches stem from the bitterness of members who remain unreconciled to the church.

It is possible to experience difficulty laying hold on the completion of forgiveness and reconciliation. It may take some time for the Lord to deal with our hearts and for us to work things out among ourselves. But as long as we are praying over that situation and working to resolve it with all of our hearts, we are living together as brothers and sisters in Christ. It is when a person closes his heart and mind to settling an issue that he cuts himself off from the church.

BROTHERS AND OTHERS

So we have these steps: If he listens to us, we've gained our brother: that's confrontation. If he won't listen, take one or two others: that's persuasion. If he won't be persuaded, tell the church: that brings in discipline. If he refuses to be reconciled, he is to be considered as an unbeliever.

How are we to treat an unbeliever? We pray for his soul. How do we treat the unsaved woman at the grocery store? We don't say, "Oh, you'll never do right. Forget you!" What do we do toward the unregenerate? Entreat them to come to God!

We may not hold unforgiveness toward a brother because he refuses to be reconciled. Some people may have the attitude, "I hope he doesn't come back to the church." Can we really allow ourselves to feel that way? What if he repented and asked to be received again? What will we call our problem with him then, a personality clash?

Fellowship

There is a difference between how a Christian is to relate to a brother who is being disciplined and an unbeliever. There are several scriptures that speak to this matter in great detail.

> Now we command you, brethren, in the name of our Lord Jesus Christ, that ye withdraw yourselves from every brother that walketh disorderly, and not after the tradition that he received of us (2 Thessalonians 3:6).

> And if any man obey not our word by this epistle, note that man and have no company with him, that

he may be ashamed. Yet count him not as an enemy, but admonish him as a brother (2 Thessalonians 3:14-15).

Here again, saints, we must grow up in our concept of forgiveness. Some things are not as either/or as we'd like for them to be. There are times that though we forgive a person, for a season he will not be a viable candidate for general fellowship with people in the church. If he has demonstrated that he is not really submitted to the church, forgive him, love him. Don't treat him as an enemy, but admonish him as a brother—and have your fellowship with other people.

Sometimes when we teach on forgiveness people become confused and try to develop fellowship again with people who are rebels. If a person is in rebellion against what the church teaches and against the leadership of the church, the scripture says we are not to have fellowship with that person that he might be ashamed. We often do not allow the power of godly shame to work in people's lives. Charles Finney called this offering people "false comfort." Rather than bringing the reality of God into their lives, we support them in their sins.

But we are not to treat them as enemies. Our attitude should be one of grief over that person who is in such a condition. Grieve over it! Don't gossip or backbite. Admonish him as a brother, "Brother, won't you please come back and make things right with the church. I'll be praying for you until you do." And by the way, forgive him. Every time you think about what he has done, loose him from your negative feelings so that God can deal with him.

I have written to you in my letter not to associate with sexually immoral people—not at all meaning the people of this world who are immoral, or the greedy and swindlers, or idolaters. In that case you would have to leave this world. But now I am writing to you that you must not associate with anyone who calls himself a brother but is sexually immoral or greedy, an idolater or a slanderer, a drunkard or a swindler. With such a man do not even eat (1 Corinthians 5:9-11 NIV).

A person is to be treated this way if he is called a *brother*. The scripture clearly says that this does not include those that are of the world, unbelievers. If we never associate with an unsaved person, we will not have much opportunity to bring them into the Kingdom. We relate to unbelievers so that we can tell them about Christ.

The enemy would like for us to become unbalanced in our understanding of forgiveness. He would like to see us all become either pharisees or humanists. Pharisees shut up the kingdom to others through unforgiveness. Humanists refuse to allow God to deal with a person through discipline that he might come to godly repentance and receive forgiveness.

Following the steps Jesus expounded in Matthew 18:15-17 insures that every member has every opportunity to be reconciled with the church. At the same time the church is protected from those elements that would undermine and destroy. The admonitions in 2 Thessalonians and 1 Corinthians provide understanding of how we can continue to forgive and help those who refuse reconciliation while preserving the integrity of the church. This Scriptural formula for forgiveness will keep our relationships with one another clean and our churches strong.

9

Final Forgiveness

Restore unto me the joy of thy salvation; and uphold
me with thy free spirit (Psalm 51:12).

If we are going to become the forgiving church
we must first walk freely as the forgiven church—
forgiven by God and by ourselves. We will never
grasp the reality of forgiving others unless and until
we learn to forgive ourselves. We know that receiving God's forgiveness is not difficult. His Word
makes this work profoundly simple: "If we confess
our sins, he is faithful and just to forgive us our
sins, and to cleanse us from all unrighteousness"
(1 John 1:9). But some Christians do have a very
real problem with forgiving themselves.

Our capacity to forgive others is directly related
to our capacity to forgive ourselves. Jesus said, "To
whom little is forgiven, the same loveth little" (Luke
7:47). It follows that the one who has received little
ministry of forgiveness will give little to others.
When we stop short in forgiving ourselves, in feeling
forgiven, then we lose the joy of our salvation. The
doubly sad end of a joyless Christian is that he no

longer converts sinners, for joy is the impetus of our testimony. "Restore unto me the joy of thy salvation ... then will I teach transgressors thy ways; and sinners shall be converted unto thee" (Psalm 51:12-13).

If we can identify the hindrances to self-forgiveness, we can secure a clear channel for God's forgiving love to flow through us to our brothers and sisters in the church and to the lost. There are three particular issues that often complicate forgiving ourselves. They deal with our view of ourselves in the past, present and future relating to our sin. Our *confidence* in ourselves is tested when we find that we were not who we thought we were. The present *consequences* of our sin constantly remind us of our failure. Feelings of *condemnation* cast doubt on our future in God's kingdom. If we can remove these obstacles to our faith we can connect the final link in the chain of communicating the forgiveness of heaven to the earth.

CONFIDENCE IN SELF

A misplaced confidence in ourselves is the antecedent to self-disappointment. We will not serve God long before we will fail Him and others in some way. How we respond to these failures will determine our future effectiveness in God's Kingdom. Peter is among those in the Bible mightily used of God in spite of great failures.

> And the Lord said, Simon, Simon, behold, Satan hath desired to have you, that he may sift you as wheat: But I have prayed for thee, that thy faith fail not: and when thou art converted, strengthen thy brethren. And [Peter] said unto him, Lord, I am ready to

go with thee, both into prison, and to death. And [Jesus] said, I tell thee, Peter, the cock shall not crow this day, before thou shalt thrice deny that thou knowest me (Luke 22:31-34).

Peter displayed his ignorance of himself when he insisted that he was ready to go with Jesus both to prison and to death. It is important for us to recognize the two attitudes presented in the above account of Peter's impending failure: Peter's self-confidence that *he would not fail*, and Jesus' unperturbed assurance that *he would fail*.

Jesus' attitude toward our potential for failure is so different from our own. He is neither surprised nor disillusioned by our shortcomings. We reveal our misplaced self-confidence when we exclaim, "I can't believe I did that," or "I don't know what made me do that." Or we sigh, "I'm so disappointed with myself."

Before I came into the ministry I could say that I had never lost a friend. I thought that this was because I knew how to get along with people. But then the Lord allowed me to be His servant and in the course of ministering God's truth I found people resisting me. Their resistance awakened feelings in me that I had not had stirred before: self-pity, fear and anger. Apparently these attitudes were in me or they couldn't have come out of me. All that we need is the right trigger to expose what is in us. It isn't that people cause us to behave in a certain way. They simply present the situation which draws a response from us that reveals our need.

We say things like, "He makes me mad." But he didn't make us anything; we make ourselves by our own chosen responses. People don't make us angry any more than they make us great. When we release ourselves in anger, it is not that something comes over us; it is that something comes out of us. We say, "I lost my temper." Tempers aren't lost; they are exercised. We meant to do it, but later discovered it wasn't wise. What we lost was self-respect, not temper.

All of the terms which we have used to shift the blame and justify ourselves when we fail must give way to the truth. The truth is that we fail because we have sin in our lives, and we need forgiveness. Forgiveness is never a problem for God: "If we confess our sins He is faithful and just to forgive us our sins." The problem comes when we are unwilling to forgive ourselves.

When we do not turn out to be who we thought we were, we are ashamed. Shame can be a very positive tool of the Holy Spirit to deal with the root of self-disappointment. That root is *pride*. Pride is expressed in two ways: we either feel superior to others or inferior to them. Both responses stem from an improper evaluation of ourselves.

Many Christians draw their evaluation of themselves not from who they are in God, but from what they do for God. This is called performance orientation. When our sense of worth and belonging is in God's grace, His unmerited favor, we are free from the ups and downs of our performances as people. The Holy Spirit is the best friend we can have to comfort us with the love of God and at the same time tell us the truth about ourselves. We can allow Him to strike this delicate balance in our hearts that will keep our failures in the proper perspective and restore us to usefulness in God's kingdom.

Knowing that we will fail and need forgiveness, Jesus has made a provision, as He said to Peter, "But I have prayed for thee, that thy faith fail not: and when thou art converted, strengthen thy brethren." When we fail it is not necessary that our faith fail with us. If we allow the ministry of forgiveness to come into our own lives, our failures will only serve to strengthen us with the result that we will be even more capable of strengthening our brothers.

The life of Peter demonstrates for us the wonderful hope of restoration. Though Peter denied Him before His crucifixion, after His resurrection Jesus publicly commissioned Peter as a leader in His infant church and to minister to His people. The only qualification that He made was that Peter love Him. "Do you love me? Feed my sheep" (John 21:17).

Do we love Him? If we have repented of our sins and received God's forgiveness, the Lord is prepared to fully restore us to His kingdom plan. His only requisite is our love.

CONSEQUENCES OF SIN

Have you ever asked yourself, "If I have really been forgiven for my sin, then why is the situation surrounding it still a problem to me?" And has the devil chimed in and said, "See there. That's proof you are not forgiven. What you did must be too big to be forgiven because things are still in a mess."

Reaping What We Sow

I have labored under this bondage myself. Though I had asked and received forgiveness from God and the people involved in a situation, every day I had to face the problem my sin had caused. Though I carried on with my responsibilities in the ministry, every day I fought the feelings of unforgiveness in my own heart. One day the Lord caused me to see the truth of the matter. He said, "I forgave you the day that you asked My forgiveness and you only have to ask Me once, but I cannot circumvent My own law that a man must reap what he sows. What is happening to you does not prove that you are unforgiven; it is merely the consequences of the problem that you caused. Don't feel guilty anymore. Forgive yourself and let the consequences humble you to give you power not to sin in that way again."

We must accept the difficulties around our failures as the lash of the loving rod of our Father and let them break us rather than accuse us. If God reversed every negative consequence of our sin, He would be breaking His own law. We do reap what we sow. But the good news is that while we are experiencing that negative harvest we can immediately start planting a righteous crop to be reaped as blessings. (I have even learned to pray that I may reap off the negative crop quickly that it will not be a hindrance to myself or others around me.)

God does not intend for the consequences of our sins to make us feel unforgiven, but we should not expect honor for enduring them. We can forgive ourselves and at the same time let the consequences humble us. Once while King David was enduring some painful consequences he said, "If I find favor in the Lord's eyes, he will bring me back and let me see [the ark] . . . let him do to me whatever seems good to him" (2 Samuel 15:25-26 NIV). David's attitude was, "I'll leave it in God's hands. I'm humbled.

If He let's me find favor, I'll minister again; if He doesn't, I won't." We cannot demand of God. We must say, "Lord, whatever you allow in my life, I receive that." David was restored as king because he put His confidence in God and allowed his sin to humble him. Let us not be like Saul who pleaded for honor in spite of his sin. "I have sinned. But please honor me before the elders of my people and before Israel" (I Samuel 15:30 NIV). Saul rejected God's way of humility and finally God rejected him.

Changing Our Perspective

Rather than weighing us down, the consequences of our sin can be of great comfort to us if we will see them from God's perspective. In the life of a Christian, discipline is the mark of sonship. "My son, do not make light of the Lord's discipline, and do not lose heart when he rebukes you, because the Lord disciplines those he loves, and he punishes everyone he accepts as a son" (Hebrews 12:5-6 NIV). What a comfort to know that not only are we forgiven, but we are beloved children of God.

We can work through the consequences of our sin with joy when we see them in relationship to the whole pattern of God's purpose for our lives. God has a plan so much bigger than the sin we have committed. If we will "come up hither" and look down on our circumstances from an eternal perspective the significance of our forgiven transgression is enormously diminished.

Even while we are going through what sometimes can be tormenting consequences, we can forgive ourselves on a daily basis. God's mercies are fresh every morning. We can allow this additional need for His grace to press us into the arms of our loving, forgiving Father.

CONDEMNATION OF SELF

Condemnation goes beyond our disappointment with ourselves and wrestling with the consequences of a particular sin. We may even feel fully forgiven for a specific sin and still labor under the oppression of condemnation. The weight of condemnation would press the life of God right out of us by having us believe that *who we are is unforgivable.* Condemnation seeks to wrap us in a winding sheet of hopelessness and bury us in a grave of despair.

It is important for us to understand the difference between the true conviction of the Holy Spirit and the condemnation that the devil aids our carnal minds in manufacturing. The Holy Spirit identifies sin in our lives. He is specific and to the point and He always accompanies His conviction of sin with the confidence of forgiveness if we will repent. We know exactly what we have done wrong and we see an immediate release through forgiveness.

Condemnation doesn't condemn sin; it condemns *us.* It calls our character into question. "Oh, you've been doing some of those kinds of things again; you know, that's what you always do. Really most of the things you've done lately haven't been right. Maybe your whole character is flawed. Yeah, that's it. You do wrong things because you are all wrong." Rather than seeing ourselves as people who fail, condemnation tells us that we are failures. We don't make mistakes, *we are one.*

Satan is not so interested in getting us to sin for the sake of the sinning. His plan is to build a super-structure of guilt on our sin. We may receive forgiveness for the sin, but the feelings of guilt hang on. After we have become enmeshed in guilt, we begin to lose confidence and faith. 1 John 3:21 says, "If our hearts do not condemn us, we have confidence before God and receive from him anything that we ask" (NIV). When we come to pray and are in condemnation we cannot ask for anything in faith or receive anything from God. Condemnation cuts off our lifeline with the Father. Thus we are locked into a seemingly unresolvable condition which precludes our usefulness to God and His purposes. As Christians we often put ourselves on "hold" because of condemnation. We need to know the full power of forgiving ourselves so that we can be put back into the harvest to labor in God's kingdom.

Deliverance from Condemnation

What is our answer to the plague of condemnation? A cry to God—deliver me from guilt! If we are delivered from something, we don't have it anymore. It doesn't mean that someone has given us some pious platitude or some promise that might work. It means that our guilt is gone. Deliverance from guilt is a part of God's restoration process.

David voiced his cry for deliverance from guilt, "Deliver me from bloodguiltiness, O God . . . and my tongue shall sing aloud of thy righteousness" (Psalm 51:14). David believed that he had been forgiven for his sins of murder and adultery, but a sense of guilt lay heavy upon him. He felt defiled by Uriah's blood.

He declares God's way for deliverance, "The sacrifices of God are a broken spirit; a broken and a contrite heart, O God, thou wilt not despise" (v. 17).

But the double vise of condemnation is that when we are caught in its grip we often erect hindrances to receiving God's means of deliverance. Instead of brokenheartedly admitting our failures to our own selves and simply agreeing with God's forgiveness, we try to atone for our sin by good works. Going to extremes to show God how sorry we are for our sins and doing good works amounts to penance. We have substituted our plan of penance for God's plan of repentance.

David stated his preference for a sacrifice, "For thou desirest not sacrifice; else I would give it; thou delightest not in burnt offering" (v. 16). When we have difficulty feeling forgiven, we would prefer to bring some animal to the sanctuary. We would rather do a good work, something that we could hold in our hand and say, "There, I did that" than to have to deal in that invisible realm in our hearts. There we are not even sure what we are looking for: "Is it stone? Is it lead? Is it still beating? How can I bring forgiveness out of it?" The Lord says that the only way to find release from the torment of condemnation is to *let our hearts break.*

We would prefer the sacrifice of good works, doing something to prove to ourselves that we are worthy. We feel that if we have done so many wrong things then we will really work at doing so many right things. We would even prefer a burnt offering. "Consume me, Lord. Do something awful to me. Punish me, but don't make me have a broken heart. Don't cause me to have to live in such a way that I am open to people."

Paul said, "Are you so foolish? After beginning with the Spirit, are you now trying to attain your goal by human effort?" (Galatians 3:3 NIV). Sometimes when we receive forgiveness from God, we try to deal with the remaining guilt by attempting to walk on doing everything exactly right. In the process we don't trust God, ourselves or anyone else. We are hardening our hearts. But God doesn't hold our sin against us. We are holding it against ourselves. We don't need a regimen of things to please God. We need deliverance from the feelings of guilt and that comes from having a contrite heart.

What is a contrite heart? How do we have one? Contrited means ground to a fine powder, or something so completely broken that it can never be put back together in the same form. When our hearts are contrited we have relinquished every trace of believing that we can please God, ourselves or other people in our own strength. We have totally given up trying and are totally trusting. All our defenses are down. We embrace our weakness and lean on God's strength. Our heart is soft—not only toward God, but toward our fellow Christians and the lost. The contrited heart is the heart of compassion.

When our hearts are contrited we ever realize the need for God and His forgiveness. We have a great testimony of His boundless love and a desire to share the knowledge of His wonderful grace. Instead of being hindered by our failures, coming to the place of heart contrition enlarges our usefulness for the kingdom.

God uses forgiven failures. There were others to choose from on the Day of Pentecost, but Jesus chose Peter, the failure, to deliver the message of the Holy

Ghost. God chose Moses, the murderer, to lead His people out of bondage. He chose David, the adulterer, to establish the line that would bring forth the Savior of the world. They only needed to accept the forgiveness God extended to them. The final forgiveness of self releases us to "be about our Father's business."

10

Forgiveness Failures

In him we have redemption through his blood, the forgiveness of sins, in accordance with the riches of God's grace" (Ephesians 1:7 NIV).

What is behind the forgiveness failure? That is the person that has read all the preceding chapters in this book and yet doesn't forgive. He usually doesn't say, "No." He says, "I can't. You don't know how awful it was in my case. I've tried and it doesn't work." The end is *he doesn't*; the command is *we must*.

When I was outlining this book I came to a point when I prayed, "It is not finished, Lord, until I have a word for that awful chapter that might even be called "Forgiveness Failures." What can I say to the person who assents to all the teaching but still does not embrace Your command to forgive? My God, anoint a chapter, some paragraphs; frame some sentences and load some words that will convict men so they might make heaven and miss hell. Lord, what is at the root of the forgiveness failure?" In answer to this petition God gave me some understanding on the nature of our difficulty in becoming the **Forgiving** Church.

THE UNFORGIVING CHURCH

The church is involved in selective forgiveness. We say, "Oh, those sinners out there are hard to love." But if we are honest we will admit that we have more difficulty loving and forgiving some Christians. The test of our forgiveness is not with unbelievers. The breakdown in forgiving is within the church among the children of God.

Why is it easy for us to forgive people in the world? Forgiving the lost makes us feel that we have fulfilled our ministry. We are waiting for the opportunity to forgive sinners. When they are saved we have succeeded as evangelists. Just give us a rotten, low-down, good-for-nothing sinner to forgive. We think this is wonderful!

But if a brother in the church becomes a dirty, rotten, low-down sinner, our response is often disgust. Forgiveness has suddenly become unforgiveness because the location of the sinner has changed. Oh, that he could have stayed in the world so he could have been forgiven when he sinned! He could have had a new start if he hadn't already been in the church!

Besides the damage done to the Christian who sins, this abuse in refusing to forgive one another in the church militates against God's command to love our brothers. Unforgiveness is a manifestation of hatred.

Do not be surprised, my brothers, if the world hates you. We know that we have passed from death to life because we love our brothers. Anyone who does not love remains in death. Anyone who hates his brother is a murderer and you know that no murderer has eternal life in him (1 John 3:13-15 NIV).

Don't be surprised, the scripture says, if the world hates you. However, as we follow the teaching, we should be shocked if Christians hate us. God calls hatred murder. Christian killing is a very dangerous sin, especially if Christians are doing the killing. There is no place for any brother in the universal Body of Christ to hate another brother; there should never be that expectation.

The scripture says that we can know that we have passed from death to life if we love our brother. Anyone who hates his brother is a murderer and does not have eternal life. Will our unforgiveness within the church cause us problems? Hellish ones. We must not deceive ourselves. God will not permit those who hold unforgiveness against their brothers to enter heaven. That's what the Bible says.

The desperation to find forgiveness within the church should weigh upon us like a man who commits adultery but seeks to be forgiven. "Can't we just have a fresh beginning? You are my wife and in God we have been commissioned and commanded to stay together. Therefore I must find forgiveness." As in marriage, Christians are in covenant with one another before God. We are obligated to find a place of reconciliation.

Why then are we willing to forgive sinners to get them into the church but begrudge forgiving them once they are our brothers and sisters? The root of this thinking lies in misunderstood redemption. We have not understood the nature of the redemption Jesus provided for us on Calvary.

REDEMPTION FOR A LIFETIME

In the beginning of his letter to the Ephesians, Paul gives a detailed explanation of what Jesus intended for us through redemption.

> For he chose us in him before the creation of the world to be holy and blameless in his sight. In love he predestined us to be adopted as his sons through Jesus Christ, in accordance with his pleasure and will—to the praise of his glorious grace, which he has freely given us in the One he loves. In him we have redemption through his blood, the forgiveness of sins, in accordance with the riches of God's grace that he lavished on us with all wisdom and understanding (Ephesians 1:4-8 NIV).

" . . . For he chose us in him before the creation of the world." Before the foundation of the world the Lamb was slain and our names were written in the Lamb's book of life. He knew that I was going to be in Shekinah Church. He knew just where He would set each member in His Body. But see what the choosing was for—not only for us to be saved and join the church.

"To be holy and blameless in his sight." God's ultimate plan is to make us holy and blameless in His sight. We're not there yet. He's working on us. The passage goes on to explain that *redemption is a process*.

"In love He predestined us to be adopted as His sons in Jesus Christ . . . In Him we have redemption through His blood, the forgiveness of sins in accordance with the riches of God's grace." Our redemption is *through His blood*, not through our consistently good behavior. The context of this whole revelation about redemption is that the blood and forgiveness provide a complete process. A. W. Tozer said, "The supreme work of Christ in redemption is not to save us from hell but to restore us to God-likeness again." [1] God is redeeming us day by day and step by step.

Here is the process of redemption: a man repents, is forgiven of his sins and enters the Kingdom of God. Now he begins a *life* of repentance and forgiveness. No matter what the offense is, who it is against, if he repents, he will be forgiven. We are continually being made holy and blameless in His sight. Redemption through the blood of Jesus comes to us through the vehicle of forgiveness.

Tozer continues, "The purpose of Christ's redeeming work was to make it possible for bad men to be able to become good—deeply, radically and finally. It became necessary not because of what men were doing, but because of what they were." [2] We say, "I've quit doing that." But we're still what we are and what we are needs redemption. What we've "quit doing" is beside the point; because of what we are we will continue to "quit doing" things all of our lives if we are maturing as Christians. If we don't want to grow and we don't want more power with God, then by all means we should hide from every situation that causes us pressure or discomfort. But if we want those things in our lives that need to be changed to be exposed, then we must allow the Holy Spirit to show us our sins. As we receive forgiveness for them we are being redeemed more and more.

Every day Jesus is buying us back from those wicked things.

Redemption is God's eternal plan. His plan for us is *redemption for a lifetime.* It's so much more than a ticket to heaven and fire insurance from hell! That shallow, solely evangelistic attitude makes no provision for the real life that we must continue living after we are saved. Many Christians have not understood that the work of redemption is progressive. In our lack of understanding we have almost made the church a revolving door where men come in by God's forgiveness of their sins and go out through our unforgiveness. Why do we persist in our rejection of His lifetime provision?

THE LONGING FOR INNOCENCE

Our human nature resists the work of redemption. If we can be delivered from the carnal mind's response to sin our attitude concerning forgiveness can be wonderfully altered. What is our first response when we realize that someone has sinned, that he did something that he should not have done? Our most common response is, "I wish he had not done that; if only that had not happened."

Now let's consider the insanity of that thought. The person sinned. It's done. But our wish is to deny that fact. People do sin. Born again Christian church members do sin. Denying the fact of sin is denying reality, and denying reality is insanity. "I wish he had not" is a place of unreality where we live in the realm of regret and refuse the work of forgiveness.

Our feelings of regret in the face of sin express our disappointment in the *need* for forgiveness. One of the main reasons we have difficulty forgiving is our desire for innocence. This desire says, "I wish I were innocent. I wish we were all innocent." I wish we had nothing that needed to be forgiven. I wish our self-righteousness were justified." God is not going to grant that wish. We are not the innocent—we are the redeemed!

Jesus redeemed us from our sins that we might have His righteousness. "For he hath made him to be sin for us, who knew no sin; that we might be made the righteousness of God in him" (2 Corinthians 5:21). The process of redemption does not make us innocent; it makes us pure. Oswald Chambers makes a clear distinction between the two.

> Purity is not innocence, it is much more. Purity is something that has been tested and tried, and triumphed; innocence always has to be shielded. Innocence in a child's life is a beautiful thing, but men and women ought not to be innocent, they ought to be tested and tried and pure. The purity God demands is impossible unless we can be re-made from within, and that is what Jesus Christ undertakes to do through the Atonement. [3]

In preferring innocence over purity, that which has no need of redemption becomes higher than that which Jesus has redeemed. In that context our own righteousness becomes greater than that of Jesus. We are saying, "I wish that we were righteous without forgiveness. I place a higher value on an unmarred life than I do a washed and restored one. I'm in the church, but I don't value redemption as highly as I do innocence. I've been made a minister of reconciliation, but I am repulsed by the fact that Jesus' blood must continually be applied for sin." Is that not trampling the blood of Jesus underfoot and despising its power? The longing for innocence is a terrible, terrible thing.

MISPLACED TRUST

We often refuse to forgive our brothers and sisters in the Lord because we say in their failing us they have violated our trust. "I never thought he would do something like that. It can never be the same between us. I just can't trust him now." In what context were we trusting him before? If we were trusting him to be perfect then we were denying the fact of sin. Our trust in people must ever be in God's redemptive power and plan for their lives. Our trust must be in Jesus' blood, not in people's infallibility.

God didn't call me into ministry because He trusted me never to sin. Can you see Jesus saying to the Father, "I am so shocked. I thought that Sue was going to be fine and upstanding in character in every situation when I called her into the ministry." He didn't think any such thing. He thought that He would call me in 1967, and that in, 1971 I was going to blow it. And in 1973 I was going to come into new revelation and in 1975 I was going to blow it worse than I did in '71. Do you know why He thought all that when He called me? Because He knew it. Not because He wanted me to blow it, but because He knew everything that I would do. Our sin doesn't surprise God. He knew every time I was going to fail—and He still entrusted me with the ministry of His Word. That's hard for our carnal minds to accept. They say, "Why didn't God call someone who wouldn't blow it?" (As in someone who was innocent!)

All of those in leadership in our church have had at least one situation in which if we had not been forgiven we could have been kicked out of ministry or really failed God and the people. Leaders don't continue in ministry in the church because we are perfect—but because we are forgiven. We remain strong in God because we keep on receiving forgiveness from people who trust in God's redemptive work in our lives.

Who did Jesus trust? "But Jesus would not entrust himself to them, for he knew all men" (John 2:24 NIV). Jesus did not trust what He knew of the hearts of men. He trusted His great ability to redeem them. Oswald Chambers said,

> [Our Lord] knows that every relationship not based on loyalty to Himself will end in disaster. Our Lord trusted no man, yet He was never suspicious, never bitter. Our Lord's confidence in God and in what His grace could do for any man, was so perfect that He despaired of no one. If our trust is placed in human beings, we shall end despairing of everyone. [4]

Forgiveness is provided because we sin! Jesus shed His blood because He knew we would. "And if any man sin, we have an advocate with the Father, Jesus Christ the righteous" (1 John 2:1). In our bid for innocence we close the door on forgiveness by denying the reality of sin.

RECONCILING THE FACT OF SIN

There are churches that do not reconcile themselves to the fact of sin so their members pretend that they don't sin! "People here will not forgive me if I sin, therefore I don't sin." The demand for innocence creates hypocrites! "You don't accept sin? Fine, I don't sin." No relationship, phoney church.

We may sincerely believe that our church is the finest group of people we've ever known, and that may be true, relatively speaking. But don't make them innocent. Make them sinners saved by grace that are going on to be redeemed—and we are going to allow it. Let them be redeemed rather than make them lie about their need for redemption.

How many happy, clappy churches are there today that are twenty feet wide and half an inch deep. They have never come to grips with the fact that Jesus Christ died because people—even Christian people—sin. They are pretending to one another, "I'm OK, you're OK" and it's all a lie. The people in the congregation are not experiencing redemption, for if someone finds out that a person has a problem or a need in his life their only answer is to write him off.

We are so flattered to go out and rescue the degraded. It's one of the social passions of mankind to offer them salvation and entrance into the Kingdom. Then later we will deny those same people the true Kingdom provision of redemption. Redemption is not just from hell when we die; it's from sin while we live. Our unforgiveness seeks to cancel a person's redemption at mid-point in his journey.

We say in effect, "I don't think that you should be redeemed anymore from this point. If Jesus wants to redeem you, that's fine, but I will not allow you to have a fresh start. As far as I am concerned you are still in the prison of your unforgiven sin." We've not realized what a terrible influence we can have on one another. What awful bondage, what terrible insecurities we can put into each others hearts. Our unforgiveness can cause people to doubt the reality of Jesus' redemption.

Religion that doesn't reconcile itself to the fact of sin destroys rather than restores. If our religion is based upon the demand for innocence, we have betrayed the blood of Jesus. We have set up a religion without a Lamb and have rejected the New Covenant. *Unforgiveness is redemption cancelled.*

GODLY DISILLUSIONMENT

When we were children we thought that our parents were perfect. They were as God to us. Somewhere along the line most of us found out that our parents had a few character flaws—and we were horribly disillusioned with them! That place of disillusionment was actually our coming out of deception. Our parents never were perfect; they were just all that we knew and we had not been exposed to all the truth. How we need to be disillusioned from our idealistic attitudes! Until we come to reality we can never minister to a real world.

I have heard people say, "I came to this church and I thought everything was wonderful and I was so happy. Then I found out that there were some people that had some problems." They were simply saying that they were happy in their ignorance and deception. If we would believe that where there are people there are problems we wouldn't have to go through such pain when we are disillusioned.

I've heard others say, "I don't know whether or

not I should stay in this church. I know too much."
They are shocked at the number of needy people in
their church and are not so sure they want to pay
the price of forgiveness to restore their brothers. In
his book *Rebuilding Your Broken World*, Gordon
MacDonald states that it is shameful for us to talk
about spiritual warfare and then act horrified when
someone is a casualty.

Once we were having some difficulties with a few
people in our church. In the course of their com-
plaining and lack of cooperation they said some
rather hurtful things about me. I began to think
back about my early days of pastoring. I remembered feeling so loved and appreciated by the congregation. Everyone shared the vision that God had
given me. They were always willing to work together
and their encouragement daily blessed me. I found
myself wishing that I still felt as I had at the beginning of my ministry.

The Lord said to me, "You felt that way then because you were deceived about the nature of people.
Now that I've allowed you to see the truth you want
to go back to that deceived state." I had been disillusioned. I had been an idealist who thought this and
that was going to happen and when it didn't I was
disillusioned. But my disillusionment was not negative! It meant that I had quit being ignorant. When
we allow disillusionment to shatter our false concepts
of one another, forgiveness can flood our souls and
we will welcome the work of redemption. Oswald
Chambers speaks of this godly disillusionment.

Disillusionment means that there are no more false
judgments in life. To be undeceived by disillusionment may leave us cynical and unkindly severe in

our judgment of others, but the disillusionment which comes from God brings us to the place where we see men and women as they really are, and yet there is no cynicism, we have no stinging bitter things to say. Many of the cruel things in life spring from the fact that we suffer from illusions. We are not true to one another as *facts*; we are true only to our *ideas* of one another. Everything is either delightful and fine, or mean and dastardly, according to our idea. [5]

FORGIVENESS FOR UNFORGIVENESS

Redemption has been given to us for a lifetime and we need forgiveness equally as long. It is right for us to be grieved when our brothers and sisters in Christ fall to sin. But as Chambers said, "If the redemption of Christ cannot go deeper down than hell, it is not redemption at all." [6] And if our forgiveness will not let people be redeemed to the uttermost then we are deceived in our understanding of Jesus' redemption.

If we can take hold of the process of redemption we can let each other out from under the feelings of accusation and the vague misery that we don't approve of one another. We really do not need each others' approval to have God's. But we can give a wonderful ministry to each other by simply saying, "My demand for innocence was not of the Kingdom of God and I didn't know it. I thank God that purity is being worked in all of us and I'm willing to forgive you so that work can continue in you."

The truth of forgiveness will set the church free. God grant us the grace to come to a true appreciation of the redemption that Jesus shed His blood for. May we allow it to every man, woman, boy and girl regardless of the stage of their maturity as Christians. And may we allow the Holy Spirit to say all that He has to say to us concerning forgiveness so that we as individuals and as churches can be freed from the tyranny of unforgiveness.

NOTES

1. *Signposts*, Harry Verploegh, editor (Wheaton, IL: Victor Books, 1988), p. 165.
2. Ibid.
3. *Oswald Chambers*, Harry Verploegh, editor (Nashville, TN: Thomas Nelson, Inc., 1987), pp. 274-275.
4. Oswald Chambers, *My Utmost for His Highest* (New York: Dodd, Mead and Company, 1935), p. 212.
5. Ibid.
6. *Oswald Chambers*, p. 281.

Prayer

Father we come before you as the Body of Christ needing so much to have Your redemptive work done in our hearts and lives. We so need to be delivered from the deception that we don't need forgiveness or that we can't give forgiveness or that there comes an end to forgiveness.

Lord, we're asking You for revelation. May the power of Your precious Holy Spirit reveal to each of us the resistance our own human nature has to the truth of the need for forgiveness. Lord, we say to You we value redemption because that was why You shed Your blood. Your blood was not shed for our innocence.

We are grateful for Your mercy on our continuing need for forgiveness of sin. You said those that are well don't need a physician. We need Your redemptive work for the sickness of sin in our lives. We will not reject the application of Your blood.

Forgive us for the deception of our carnal minds that demands innocence and refuses forgiveness, that grows weary with the ongoing need for forgiveness because we grow weary of the redemption plan. Oh God, forgive us when we have desired to cut off our brothers and sisters at mid-point in their walk with You and thwart Your plan to fully reconcile them to Your whole purpose. We repent as Your church saying, Lord, cleanse us from unforgiveness. We need forgiveness for our unforgiveness. And we rejoice in Your redemption as we receive Your forgiveness.

Books by Sue Curran

Available from
Shekinah Publishing Company

KINGDOM PRINCIPLES

This book contains the basic Scriptural principles
upon which Shekinah was established. It has been
translated into many languages and enjoys wide circulation throughout the world as a foundational
study course (textbook) for those who desire to be
established in sound doctrine and to grow in Jesus
Christ.

THE PRAYING CHURCH

In 1980 Shekinah experienced a sovereign move of
the Holy Spirit in which the church gathered in
daily corporate prayer morning and evening for four
months. This intense visitation of God's Spirit established a corporate prayer life that remains the
strength of the work. *The Praying Church* gives the
Scriptural principles and historical background of
corporate prayer and clearly addresses practical
aspects of the prayer meeting: maintaining life, faith
and unity; overcoming hindrances; leading in prayer.
This handbook for corporate praying has been translated into several languages and has found international circulation.

For a complete list of tapes and books
by Sue Curran
and other materials available from
Shekinah Church Ministries, write:

Shekinah Publishers
394 Glory Road
Blountville, TN 37617